Rock Formations

Text edited in the UK by Tregaron Press, Tregaron, Wales SY25 6JF. **info@markmywords.co.uk**

Cover art and design by Mayapriya Long of Bookwrights. **www.bookwrights.com**

For further information contact Cidermill Books:- **info@cidermillbooks.com**

ISBN 0-9748483-5-2 (Paperback Version)

2004111420

Rock Formations

Categorical Answers To How Band Names Were Formed

Dave Wilson

Cidermill Books

For Carole

Contents

Contents

Contents

Contents

Acknowledgements

Thanks are due to the following people for their assistance and support in making this book possible:

Information:

      Rachel Sadler

      Claire Richards

      James Dupre

Content editing:

      James Dupre

      Fintan Healy

      Keith Britton

      Bev Richards

Cover art:

      Mayapariya Long of Bookwrights.

Copyediting:

> Paul Ingrams of Tregaron Press, Wales (whose father, Michael Ingrams, is mentioned in the entry for **Michael Crawford**)

Indexing:

> Claire Richards

Cheerleading:

> Bev Richards

> Ann McKim

Most importantly, I would like to thank my wife Bev for her unwavering support, suggestions, extremely time consuming content editing and IT skills.

Preface

I was unsure how long I'd been researching this book, until recently I came across an early electronic copy on floppy disk–the date stamp was March 1995. So its been at least nine years.

The band name that started me on this journey was Steely Dan–I was rather surprised by the origin (see the chapter entitled "Ooh, La La!")–but this had me looking into other seemingly strange names, and it took off from there. Having been employed full-time during that period (or at least for most of it), it hasn't been easy to spend as much time as I would have liked on research. Nonetheless, my wife can attest to me having spent countless hours researching (even in the bathroom with armloads of music reference books). My notes were never far away–I remember cataloging this book in places as far apart as Calgary and Tashkent!

For the first four years of research, I was living in the UK; for the last five, I have been resident in California. I hope this has allowed me to produce a reference that is equally interesting to readers on both sides of the pond.

This is one of those projects that can never be finished, as there exist thousands and thousands of established acts, and of course there are always new acts coming to prominence.

Thanks for investing your time and money to allow me to share what became a long-term passion with me. I hope this book gives you as much enjoyment reading it as I had researching it.

Finally, I am proud to say that I have written a book on band names without once including that over-used word "moniker"!

Dave Wilson, San Jose, CA
March 2004

Introduction

First, a confession; the book title, Rock Formations, is admittedly a bit of a misnomer, as there are entries covering the whole spectrum of popular music, including for example jazz and blues artists of the early twentieth century. However, I originally intended to include only rock music entries, and thought up the snappy title with that in mind. Once I expanded the scope of the book, I decided to stick with the snappy title–I hope you don't mind!

I decided not to make this just another dictionary-type reference, with page after page of alphabetical entries. Instead, I noted that many of the entries had a lot in common and decided to group them into appropriate categories, e.g. movies, places, etc. I hope the reader appreciates this slight deviation from the norm. Entries within the various categories are however listed alphabetically for convenience.

To aid the reader in locating a particular entry within the various categories, there is a complete index at the back of the book; artists and groups that have their own entry are shown in UPPERCASE, and also have the page for their entry shown in bold type. This allows the reader to use the index to find which names share a particular influence, e.g. **The Beatles**.

Where a name could have been included in more than one category, these have been placed in the most appropriate one.

In the category "Nom de Plume", I have included one or two artists who record under their real names, where I feel there is some additional interest to the reader.

Where there were disagreements in the information that I found during my researches, I have left the last word to the artists themselves, where this is available.

The Conventions

No, that isn't the name of a 'sixties soul band (although perhaps it should have been). I have used the following conventions throughout the book:-

Cross-references: groups or artists having their own entry and which are referenced within a different entry are shown in bold font.

"Song Titles": song titles are shown in quotation marks.

Other Titles: Album titles, book titles, movie titles and TV shows are shown in italics. Album titles are also accompanied by the original year of release.

Instruments: the instruments played by the various artists and group members, i.e. vocals, guitars, bass, drums, keyboards, etc. are shown in full.

Real names: real names are sometimes listed with the prefix "*b.*", the abbreviation for "born". Note: Where band members have adopted a stage name, this information is included under the entry for the particular band, except where they went on to solo success, e.g. **Sting**.

Warning/Disclaimer

This book is designed to provide information on the origins of group and artist stage names. It is not the purpose of this book to provide full biographical details on those acts that have been included.

Every effort has been made to make this reference book as complete and as accurate as possible. However, despite the best efforts of the author and the various people involved in editing this book, there may be mistakes, both typographical and in content. Therefore the information contained herein should be used as a guide and not as the ultimate source of information. Furthermore, this book contains information that was current at the time of going to press.

The purpose of this book is to inform and entertain. The author and Cidermill Books shall have neither liability nor responsibility to any person or entity with respect to any loss or damage caused, or alleged to have been caused, directly or indirectly, by the information contained in this book. If you do not wish to be bound by the above, you may return this book to the publisher for a full refund.

Lights, Camera, Action!

Bands and artists whose names were
inspired by movies or movie titles

? & The Mysterians

Group leader "?" used the name Rudy Martinez to collect royalties, although there is some doubt that it is his real name. "Mysterians" came from the low-budget Japanese sci-fi movie *The Mysterians* (1957), directed by Ishiro Honda (sometimes referenced as *Inoshiro* Honda), who achieved fame as director of the original Godzilla movies.

10,000 Maniacs

Originally formed as Still Life, the new name was inspired by the title of a B-movie directed by Herschell Gordon Lewis, and starring Jeffrey Allen, Connie Mason and Thomas Wood. The movie was actually titled *2,000 Maniacs* (1965), a cult film based on the play *Brigadoon* (about the Scottish village that only appears once each century) and was originally to have been titled "5,000 Maniacs". The band name was suggested by John Lombardo (guitars) on joining the band. Everyone accepted that "10,000 Maniacs" was the actual title of the movie when in fact no one in the band had seen it.

All About Eve

After first rejecting the name Electric Funeral and Red Red Wound, the group's final name was taken from the title of the Joseph L Mankiewicz 1950 movie classic *All About Eve* starring Bette Davis and Anne Baxter, itself based on the play *The Wisdom of Eve* by Mary Orr.

Alphaville

Alphaville was the title of a 1965 French science-fiction film directed by Jean-Luc Godard and starring Eddie Constantine and Anna Karina. The band liked the movie, particularly leading man Constantine. Interestingly, a different band was already using the name "Alphaville" in Spain, necessitating a label change in that country alone by the more famous Alphaville.

Army Of Lovers

The group's name was chosen by the bisexual leader of the group, Alexander Bard, and was inspired by the title of a German cult film *Armee der Liebenden, oder Revolte der Perversen* (1978) ("Army of Lovers, or Revolution of the Perverts"), directed by Gay Rights activist and filmmaker Rosa von Praunheim. Vocalist La Camilla (*b.* Camilla Henemark).

Bad Company

Bad Company was the title of a 1972 Robert Benton-directed Civil War western starring Jeff Bridges, and was suggested by vocalist Paul Rodgers. It was initially the title of a song he had written with Simon Kirke, prior to the band choosing a name. **Led Zeppelin's** label Swan Song tried to get them to change the name on signing them, considering it to be too dangerous-sounding, but the band refused.

Afrika Bambaata

Afrika Bambaata was born Kevin Donovan, and his stage name is shortened from Afrika Bambaata Aasim, the name of a 19th-century Zulu chief featured in the movie *Zulu* (1964), directed by Cy Endfield and starring Stanley Baker. The name translates as "Chief Affection".

Blues Traveler

The name Blues Traveler has two sources of inspiration, both involving movies starring Dan Aykroyd, of whom the group are big fans (Aykroyd has appeared on stage with the band several times). One source is *The Blues Brothers* (1980), directed by John Landis, and the other is Gozer the Traveler, a character mentioned in *Ghostbusters* (1984), directed by Ivan Reitman.

Boomtown Rats

Originally known as the Nightlife Thugs, the Boomtown Rats took their name from a gang of Oklahoma kids who were offspring of oil-well laborers, featured in the 1976 movie *Bound for Glory*, directed by Hal Ashby and starring David Carradine. The movie is based on Woody Guthrie's autobiography of the same name. Johnny Fingers (keyboards–*b*. John Moylett); Pete Briquette (bass–*b*. Patrick Cusack).

Commander Cody & The Lost Planet Airmen

This band was named by band member George Frayne (AKA Commander Cody), who says the inspiration came from a '50s movie called "Commander Cody and The Lost Planet Airmen", starring Kristen Coffen as Kommando Kody. In fact, the band did a promo with Coffen some years after their formation. However, it's likely that the inspiration was a mixture of *Commando Cody* (featured in a 12-chapter series of movies in the early '50s, none of which included "Lost Planet Airmen" in the title), and a late 1940's movie named *Lost Planet Airmen*, directed by Fred Brannon and starring Tristram (not Kristen) Coffin.

Counting Crows

Counting Crows took their name from an old English divination rhyme, comparing the pointlessness of life with the act of counting crows. The poem was quoted in one of vocalist Adam Duritz's girlfriend Mary-Louise Parker's films *Signs Of Life* (1989), directed by John David Coles.

Actually, the original poem (which is an old English folk poem) refers to counting magpies rather than crows (it was also adapted in the title song of '70s UK children's TV series *Magpie*), and is supposed to tell the future of someone who sees a flock of magpies, depending on how many birds make up the flock:

> One for sorrow, two for mirth,
> Three for a wedding, four for a birth,
> Five for silver, six for gold,
> Seven for a secret not to be told
> Eight for heaven, nine for hell
> And ten for the devil's own sel'.
> (Trad.)

Divine

Born Harris Glenn Milstead, the "Divine" character was created by him and movie director John Waters for the 1966 movie *Roman Candles*. Milstead adopted the name full-time after opening a nostalgia store called "Divine Trash" in Providencetown, Mass.

Duran Duran

After first rejecting the name RAF (the abbreviation for the UK Royal Air Force), the group's final name was suggested by bass player John Taylor during a brainstorming session with keyboard player Nick Rhodes, and was taken from the character played by Milo O'Shea (actually the character's name is "Durand Durand") in the sci-fi movie *Barbarella* (1968), starring Jane Fonda and directed by Dino de Laurentiis. Coincidentally, some early gigs were played at a venue named Barbarella's in Birmingham, UK where they were formed. Nick Rhodes (keyboards–b. Nicholas Bates), changed his name for "aesthetic" purposes, and his new surname "Rhodes" was also suggested by John Taylor.

Fine Young Cannibals

Fine Young Cannibals were named at random from a movie book, after the 1960 film *All The Fine Young Cannibals*, directed by Michael Anderson and starring Natalie Wood and Robert Wagner.

Bobby Gentry

Born Roberta "Bobby Lee" Streeter, Gentry took her stage name from the film *Ruby Gentry* (1952), directed by King Vidor and starring Jennifer Jones and Charlton Heston.

Kid Creole

Born Thomas August Darnell Browder (later shortened to August Darnell), he adopted the stage name alias "Kid Creole" after *King Creole*, the 1958 film directed by Michael Curtiz and starring Elvis Presley. By 1985, he had self-appointed himself King Creole and began using that name instead of Kid Creole.

Klaatu

This name came from a phrase ("Klaatu Barada Nikto") spoken in the 1951 sci-fi movie *The Day The Earth Stood Still*, directed by Robert Wise. Michael Rennie's character, Klaatu, instructed Helen Benson (played by Patricia Neal) to say this in order to prevent the robot Gort from destroying the Earth. The band had seen the movie, liked it and identified with Klaatu, the central character played by Rennie. Incidentally, the band was originally rumored to have been the reformed Beatles, which at first they made no effort to deny.

Mindbenders

This was suggested by front man **Wayne Fontana**, and is the title of a 1963 horror film directed by Basil Dearden and starring Dirk Bogarde, which was playing at the local cinema at the time the group was formed.

Orb

This name was taken from the phrase "The orb, the orb, give me the orb", referring to a pleasure device in Woody Allen's movie, *Sleeper* (1973). Dr Alex Paterson, founder member, was born Duncan Robert Alex Paterson (hence the use of DR as a prefix).

Quireboys

The Quireboys were initially formed as *The Choirboys*, after a 1978 movie they had seen, starring Charles Durning and James Woods and directed by Robert Aldrich. Construction worker colleagues of band members Spike Gray and Guy Bailey suggested they change the name to The Queerboys, as a disparaging comment on their image. Their final name was adopted after the name "Queerboys" caused crowd problems at early gigs, and also to help in getting them accepted onto the bill of the 1986 Reading Festival in the UK.

Searchers

The Searchers were named after the 1956 western of the same name and directed by John Ford, starring John Wayne. Mike Pender (vocals, guitars–*b*. Michael Prendergast); Chris Curtis (drums–*b*. Christopher Crummy).

Siouxsie & The Banshees

Siouxsie Sioux (*b.* Susan Dallion) took inspiration for her name from Native-American Indians (she hated cowboys), and the group name "Banshees" was taken from the 1970 horror film *Cry of the Banshee*, starring Vincent Price and directed by Gordon Hessler. Budgie (drums–*b.* Peter Clarke).

Terrorvision

Originally known as Spoilt Bratz, Terrorvision took their final name from a 1986 sci-fi movie called *Terror Vision*, directed by Ted Nicolaou and starring Diane Franklin.

Texas

Texas took their name from Wim Wenders' 1984 movie *Paris, Texas* starring Sam Shephard, as band members Ally McErlaine (guitars) and Sharleen Spiteri (vocals) were particularly fond of Ry Cooder's slide guitar-based sound-track.

They Might Be Giants

They Might Be Giants is the name of a 1971 film directed by Anthony Harvey and starring George C. Scott and Joanne Woodward. It had initially been used as a stage name by a ventriloquist friend of the band, who offered the use of the name to the group after deciding to quit the business. In the movie, the main character thinks he is Sherlock Holmes, and at one point he makes reference to the novel *Don Quixote de la Mancha*, by Miguel de Cervantes, in that considering all windmills to be giants is insanity, but to think that they might be giants, i.e. to question what is generally accepted, is the root of all genius. Band member John Linnell has said that the group is "Quixotic", describing it as either an exercise in futility or a noble quest.

Utah Saints

This name was inspired by the last line of the film *Raising Arizona* (1987) directed by Joel Coen and starring Nicholas Cage. The line mentions Utah, and is spoken over a dream sequence supposedly set in the future. The band members added "Saints" to give the name more of a group feel.

Veruca Salt

Veruca Salt was named after the spoiled little girl in the children's novel *Charlie and the Chocolate Factory* by Roald Dahl. The book was subsequently made into a movie entitled *Willie Wonka and the Chocolate Factory* (1971), directed by Mel Stuart and starring Gene Wilder as Willie Wonka, with the character of Veruca Salt played by Julie Dawn Cole.

Johnny "Guitar" Watson

Born John Watson, the nickname "Guitar" was inspired by the western movie *Johnny Guitar* (1954), directed by Nicholas Ray and starring Joan Crawford and Sterling Hayden. Watson had seen the movie with his record label owner, Joe Bihari.

White Zombie

White Zombie comes from the Bela Lugosi horror movie of the same name, made in 1932 and directed by Victor Halperin. Band leader Rob Zombie was born Robert

Cummings, first adopting the stage name Robert Straker because he didn't think the name Cummings sounded evil enough.

Author! Author!

Bands whose names were inspired
by books and authors

Amboy Dukes

Founder member Ted Nugent had become aware of a previous Detroit band which had used this name, so he decided to use the name for his own group on moving from Detroit to Chicago. The name *Amboy Dukes* originates from a 1942 pulp novel about Brooklyn street gangs, written by Irving Shulman, although Nugent has stated that he has never read the book.

Beat

This name was taken from the music section of *Roget's Thesaurus* by vocalist/guitarist Dave Wakelin. The band was known as English Beat in the US to avoid a clash with another group of the same name.

Better Than Ezra

The name allegedly came from page 96 of Earnest Hemingway's book *A Movable Feast* (1964) (a reference to poet Ezra Pound). Another source claims that one of the band members was disappointed at not being accepted by Cornell University, which was founded by Ezra Cornell and that he was "better than Ezra". The band refuses to confirm which (if any) is correct, and in fact claim that not even their wives know the true story!

Boo Radleys

The Boo Radleys were named after the shady character "Boo Radley" in Harper Lee's novel *To Kill A Mockingbird* (1960). The name was chosen one night in a pub, and was inspired by the fact that they had studied the book in school and liked the sound of the character's name. Sice (guitars/vocals–b. Simon Rowbottom) recorded as Eggman.

Collective Soul

Band member Ed Roland (vocals, guitars) had seen the term "collective soul" (i.e. applying the concept of a soul to the whole of mankind) when he read *The Fountainhead* by Ayn Rand, and it had always stuck with him.

Crickets

This name was suggested by group member Jerry Allison after reading the insect section of an encyclopedia. Apparently the group at one time even considered calling themselves The Beetles!

Destiny's Child

The name Destiny's Child developed from the initial suggestion of "Destiny" by group member Beyonce Knowle's mother, having been inspired by a passage in the book of Isaiah in the *Bible* (Isaiah 65:11 contains the words "But as for you who forsake the Lord and forget my holy mountain, who spread a table for Fortune and fill bowls of mixed wine for Destiny..."). On the discovery that Destiny was already taken as a band name, Beyonce's father suggested adding the word "Child".

Eyeless In Gaza

Eyeless In Gaza is the title of a 1936 novel on the subject of pacifism by Aldous Huxley, a hero of band member Martyn Bates. The book's title refers to the biblical story of Samson, who was blinded after being taken to the Philistines' slave city, Gaza.

Fall

This name is taken from the Albert Camus novel, *The Fall*, published originally as *La Chute* in France in 1956, and was suggested by band member Tony Friel. Mark E Smith (vocals–*b*. Mark Edward Smith).

Fugs

"Fug" was a term used by Norman Mailer in *The Naked and the Dead* (1948), as an acceptable alternative for the word "fuck", and was suggested as a group name by group member Tuli Kupferberg.

Gaye Bikers On Acid

Gaye Bikers On Acid was the name of a cartoon by noted album cover and magazine artist Ray Lowry. Mary Mary (vocals–*b*. Ian Garfield Hoxley) was initially known as Mary Millington, after the tragic 1970s British porn star; Robber (bass–*b*. Ian Michael Reynolds); Rocket Ronnie (DJ–*b*. William Samuel Ronald Monroe).

Generation X

Generation X was the title of a 1964 paperback by Chris Hamblett and Jane Davidson, concerning '60s UK youth movements known as Mods and Rockers. The book was found by bassist Tony James in Billy Idol's bedroom, so James suggested using the title as the name of the band they were forming.

Grateful Dead

Grateful Dead is the name given to a kind of traditional folk tale, whereby someone pays off a dead man's debts and is later miraculously rewarded (by the "grateful dead"). Founder member Jerry Garcia (vocals, guitars), having discovered that their original name The Warlocks was already being used and so looking for a replacement name at the time, came across the term while browsing a dictionary at bassist Phil Lesh's house. Garcia has been quoted as saying that the moment of discovery was like a mystical experience for him, where everything else faded away to leave just those words on the page. The name has also been attributed to a quote from the *Egyptian Book Of The Dead*, but this was likely found after the band was already named. Some references mention that the "grateful dead" was a type of ballad collected by 19th-century music historian Francis Child, though there are no ballads with that name listed in any of his works. The band did however perform some ballads (e.g. "Barbara Allen") which are found in Child's collection *English and Scottish Popular Ballads* (5 volumes, 1882–1898).

Heaven 17

Heaven 17 was the name of a band invented by novelist Anthony Burgess, and featured in his book, *A Clockwork Orange*. The band is listed, with the song title "Inside", as part of a record chart posted in a store in Stanley Kubrick's movie version of the book.

House Of Love

This name is taken from a novel by Anais Nin, called *A Spy In The House Of Love* (1959), the sleeve of which is visible on the cover of their compilation album *Spy In The House Of Love* (1990).

Icicle Works

This name is taken from the title of Frederick Pohl's science fiction book, *The Day The Icicle Works Closed* (1959), a novel about the misuse of political power.

Joy Division

The name Joy Division was suggested by vocalist Ian Curtis, and was the name given to the particular group of concentration camp barracks where women were kept to entertain the Nazi soldiers. The term was found in Karol Cetinsky's book *House of Dolls*, detailing his families experience of the Holocaust and written under his camp name and number, Ka-Tzetnik #135633. The group quotes from the book in their song "No Love Lost" which was featured on the 1978 EP *An Ideal For Living*. Originally called Warsaw, from David Bowie's track "Warszawa" on the album *Low* (1977), this had to be changed to avoid confusion with London punk band, Warsaw Pakt. Band member Bernard Albrecht (*b.* Bernard Summer AKA Bernard Dicken) has changed his name on occasion for undisclosed family reasons.

Level 42

The inspiration for this name, rather than being a large multi-story car park, was in fact Douglas Adams' science fiction comedy novel *The Hitchhikers Guide to the Galaxy*, in which "42" (which was to have been the band's original name) is the answer to the ultimate question of the meaning of life, the universe and everything. The band decided to add "Level" before they began recording. Boon Gould (guitars–*b.* Roland Gould).

Manhattan Transfer

Manhattan Transfer was originally formed in New York in 1969, taking their name from the book of the same name by John Dos Passos. After the first line-up split, original vocalist Tim Hauser reformed the group and retained the same name.

Marillion

Marillion were originally called *Silmarillion*, after the novel of that title by *Lord Of The Rings* author, J.R.R. Tolkein, which happened to be lying around when they were deciding on a name. This was later shortened to Marillion to avoid copyright issues. Fish (vocals–b. Derek William Dick) acquired his nickname while staying at a boarding house where the landlady would charge him for each bath, so he stayed in the water as long as possible to get his money's worth.

Mott The Hoople

Group manager Guy Stevens had read *Mott The Hoople*, a 1967 novel by Willard Manus, while serving time in jail, and he it was who suggested that the band use the book title as their name.

Mungo Jerry

Mungojerrie is the name of a character in T.S. Eliot's *Old Possum's Book of Practical Cats* (1939), which was later used as the basis of the musical, *Cats*. The name was pulled out at random from a selection, where it had been wrongly spelt as two separate words, which the band decided to keep.

New Riders Of The Purple Sage

A country & western band called *Riders Of The Purple Sage* formed in the 1930's, took their name from the title of the 1912 Zane Gray western novel. Towards the end of the 1960's, Grateful Dead founder member Jerry Garcia formed a band called New Riders Of The Purple Sage, under the mistaken impression that the members of the older band were all dead, a fact which was refuted by Buck

Page of the original band on meeting Garcia! Page in fact went on to appear on stage with the (new) New Riders on several occasions.

Primal Scream

This name was inspired by Arthur Janov's "Primal Scream" therapy (part of the therapy is known as **Tears for Fears**), as featured in his book, *Prisoners of Pain* (1980). Band member Bobby Gillespie had heard the term when he was younger, and he has also said that the name is additionally a tribute to John Lennon's 1970 album *John Lennon/Plastic Ono Band*, composed after John and Yoko had undergone the therapy with Janov himself and often referred to as Lennon's "Primal Scream" album. Throb (guitars–b. Robert Young), Mani (bass–b. Gary Mounfield).

Savage Garden

Savage Garden is taken from a concept set out in the Anne Rice novel *The Vampire Lestat*, in which she writes that the vampire's world is both a beautiful and a savage garden. The group thought this description was appropriate to them.

Sixpence None The Richer

A Christian band, their name is taken from a term used to summarize an analogy used by C.S. Lewis in his book *Mere Christianity*, and was suggested by guitarist Matt Slocum. The analogy is that a father is asked by his child for a sixpence to buy him a birthday present, and although he is pleased with the gift, only an idiot would think the father is sixpence to the good on the transaction (Lewis did not use the actual phrase "sixpence none the richer" in his original work). The analogy is meant to relate that God has given humanity the gift of life, and that worship is merely returning His original gift.

Soft Machine

The Soft Machine (1961) was the title of a novel by William Burroughs, and the band's use of the name was inspired by founder member Daevid Allen's connection with Burroughs, the two having lived in the same hotel (The Beat Hotel) on France's Left Bank. Incidentally, this book also first coined the phrase "heavy metal", being a term for addictive drugs.

Spirit

Spirits Rebellious, the bands original name, was the title of a 1908 book by Kahlil Gibran, although this name was later shortened to Spirit. Randy California (guitars–b. Randolph Wolfe in Los Angeles, California), was given his nickname by Jimi Hendrix, and subsequently adopted it as his stage name.

Steppenwolf

Steppenwolf was the title of a 1927 novel by Herman Hesse, and was suggested by producer Gabriel Mekler as a change from their original name, The Sparrow. John Kay (vocals, guitars–b. Joachim Krauledat) escaped from East Germany with his mother as a child, then moved to Canada, where he anglicized his name; Nick St Nicholas (bass–b. Nicholas Kassbaum); Goldy McJohn (keyboards–b. John Goadsby) changed his name as it was decided that they didn't want two people called John in the group; Jerry Edmonton (drums–b. Jerry McCrohan), changed his name to Edmonton so as to sound more English, this being at the height of the so-called mid–'60s "British Invasion", as did his brother and ex-Sparrow member Dennis, the composer of the classic "Born To Be Wild". Dennis later enjoyed a degree of solo success as Mars Bonfire.

Supertramp

This name was inspired by the 1908 book *The Autobiography of a Supertramp*, by W. H. Davies, in which he describes his life as a hobo (tramp). The name was suggested by the band's sax player Dave Winthorp.

Tears For Fears

This name was taken from Arthur Janov's book on **Primal Scream** therapy, *Prisoners of Pain* (1980). The therapy aims to get rid of childhood anxieties by exchanging "tears for fears". Both group members were interested in Janov's work, and their 1983 album The Hurting is heavily inspired by Janov, including a track called "Prisoners of Pain". Roland Orzabal (vocals, guitars–*b*. Roland Orzabal de la Quintana)

Tubes

Tubes was shortened from the original suggestion "Tubes, Rods and Bulbs", found by the band in a medical dictionary and referring to the bones of the inner ear. Fee Waybill (vocals–*b*. John Waldo Waybill).

Uriah Heep

The band were looking for a new name around Christmas 1969, which happened to be the 100th anniversary of the death of Charles Dickens. This meant that his name was very prominent at the time, leading to band manager Gerry Bron suggesting the name of a character in Dickens' novel *David Copperfield* as the band's name.

Hot Off The Press

Bands and artists whose names were inspired
by newspapers and magazines

Bachman-Turner Overdrive

The first part of the band name comes from the two leaders of the band, Randy Bachman and Fred Turner, while the last part is from a US truckers' magazine called *Overdrive* which the band had seen while on tour. "Overdrive" was considered appropriate as they were in the process of changing their style from country rock to a harder rock style. The magazine also inspired the group's "gearwheel" logo, which was designed by band member Robin Bachman (drums).

Bonzo Dog Doo-Dah Band

The band was originally called The Bonzo Dog Dada Band, after a session spent writing words on pieces of paper to come up with ideas for a name for the group. Singer Viv Stanshall had written Bonzo Dog on one piece of paper, as he liked the cartoon puppy dog created by George Studdy and featured for many years in the English newspaper *The Daily Sketch*, while someone else had written "dada" after the Dadaist surrealist art movement. Dada was changed to Doo-Dah to avoid misunderstanding.

Buzzcocks

Band member Howard Devoto saw a review of *Rock Follies*, the UK ITV television series about the adventures of an all-girl group, in London's *Time Out* magazine. The review ended with the words "Its the buzz, cock", "cock" in this context being an English colloquialism equivalent to "mate" or "pal". Pete Shelley (vocals) changed his name from Peter McNeish, because Shelley was to have been his first name had he been born female. Howard Devoto (vocals) was born Howard Trafford, and although "devoto" is Latin for "bewitching", he actually took the name from that of a Cambridge bus driver who was featured in an after-dinner story narrated by a philosophy tutor.

Clash

The name Clash was taken from a headline in the newspaper *The London Evening Standard*, spotted by band member Paul Simenon. Joe Strummer (guitars–*b*. John Mellor) earlier used the name Woody Mellor (in honor of Woody Guthrie), becoming Joe Strummer on forming The 101ers, named after the address of a squat in London's Maida Hill district.

Bing Crosby

Born Harry Lillis Crosby, the nickname "Bing" came from *The Bingville Bugle*, a comic strip in the local Sunday paper which an older friend, Valentine Hobart, would read to him. Hobart nicknamed him "Bingo from Bingville", which eventually got shortened to "Bing".

Cult

Originally Southern Death Cult, from a newspaper headline seen by vocalist Ian Astbury (*b*. Ian Lindsay), their name was later shortened to Cult. The Southern Death Cult was a tribe who worshipped death in Mississippi around AD400. Drummer Mark Brzezicki was dubbed "Mark Unpronounceablename" in the UK pop magazine *Smash Hits*.

Daft Punk

Daft Punk were originally called Darlin' after **The Beach Boys** song of the same name. They were subsequently described by UK rock music paper *Melody Maker* as "Daft Punk" and adopted that name in retribution, as the article had been highly critical.

Depeche Mode

Depeche Mode was the name of a French fashion magazine, and translates as "Fashion Dispatch" (not "Fast Fashion" as is usually reported). Members of the band had seen the magazine and liked the sound of the phrase (band member Vince Clarke was previously in a band called French Look when he first met future Depeche Mode singer Dave Gahan).

Dishwalla

Originally named Dish, they were forced to change on the discovery of an existing band with that name. The new name was taken from an article seen in *Wired* magazine about street merchants selling satellite dishes in India, known locally as "dishwallas".

Goo Goo Dolls

Early on, they were told by a local venue promoter that he would only book them on condition they changed their name from The Sex Maggots. The new name, which is not related to Goo-Goos candy, was taken from a *True Detective* magazine advertisement for a doll's head into which you inserted your finger to change its expression.

Love and Rockets

Love and Rockets is the name of a series of alternative comic books created by Jaime and Gilberto Hernandez, based particularly on LA Mexican-American culture. The band used the name without permission and, in retaliation, Gilberto Hernandez parodied a bad garage band named Love and Rockets in the comic *Love And Rockets X*, published in 1993.

Megadeth

US Senator Alan Cranston used the phrase "The arsenal of megadeath cannot be rid" in a speech referring to the large number of deaths after a nuclear strike. Band member Dave Mustaine saw the phrase in an article he was reading on a plane and was impressed by it, incorporating it into his song "Set The World Afire", and an early member of the band suggested using "Megadeth" as the band's name.

Pop Will Eat Itself

This rather odd phrase was seen in an article by David Quantick in the UK music paper *NME (New Musical Express)*. The article concerned the group Jamie Wednesday (who later changed their name to **Carter USM**) and was discussing how pop music ideas are constantly being recycled, ending with the phrase "pop will eat itself".

Pulp

Singer Jarvis Cocker was browsing a copy of the UK finance newspaper, *The Financial Times*, during an Economics lesson at school, looking for a name for his band. He came across "Arabicus Pulp" in the commodities listing, so the band initially adopted that as its name, before later shortening it to Pulp, Arabicus Pulp being too much of a mouthful. Cocker later said that he had originally wanted to use just Pulp anyway, but that at the time it seemed too short.

Ratt

The original name Mickey Ratt came from a comic book character (actually "Mickey Rat") created, originally as a t-shirt design, by underground artist Robert Armstrong. They later shortened the name to Ratt after he objected.

Rufus

Rufus were originally named Ask Rufus, from the *Mechanics Illustrated* advice column of the same name, however this was later shortened.

Teardrop Explodes

This name was seen by the band in a 1971 *Daredevil* comic from Marvel. The scene shows an android crying, and the various frames on the page follow the tear as it falls, ending with the caption, "The teardrop explodes".

Thin Lizzy

The band were looking for a name, and during the course of things they were scanning children's comics, when guitarist Eric Bell suggested Tin Lizzie, being the name of a female robot in the UK children's comic, *The Beano*. The spelling was then changed to Thin Lizzy, because in Ireland, where they were formed, "Thin" would be pronounced as "Tin".

X-Ray Spex

X-Ray Spex comes from the cheap gadget glasses advertised in DC Comics, which allegedly enabled the wearer to see through objects. Poly Styrene (vocals–*b.* Marion Elliot), Jak Airport (guitars–*b.* Jack Stafford), Chris Chrysler (drums–*AKA* BP ("Big" Paul) Hurding), Lora Logic (sax–*b.* Susan Whitby).

Media Darlings

Bands and artists whose names were
inspired by TV & radio shows

Ant & Dec

Born respectively Anthony McPartlin and Declan Donnelly, Ant & Dec originally recorded as PJ & Duncan, which were the names of the characters they played in BBC TV's children's drama, *Byker Grove*.

Archies

The Archies were a gang of kids featured in a children's cartoon TV show, in which the song "Sugar, Sugar" was first heard. This song was subsequently released as a single and credited to The Archies. The cartoon show was based on comic strip characters created by Bob Montana, which in turn were based on high school characters known to him–the main character Archie was based on popular teen radio star Henry Aldrich.

Bananarama

Bananarama's name is jointly inspired by the children's TV show *Banana Splits* and **Roxy Music's** hit "Pajama Rama". It was intended that the name would give the group a bright, summery approach.

Boney M

Boney M was named for the main character in the Australian TV detective show *Boney*, played by Buddy Ebsen (most famous for playing the part of Jed Clampett in TV's The Beverley Hillbillies).

Crash Test Dummies

This name was suggested by a friend at medical school, although not seriously, and came from the US TV ad campaign to promote the wearing of seat belts, featuring living crash test dummies.

Credence Clearwater Revival

Credence Clearwater Revival was originally known as The Golliwogs, while their final name was a combination of the name of a friend of the band (Credence Nuball), an Olympia beer TV commercial (Clearwater) and Revival as in re-hashing The Golliwogs.

Department S

This band was named after *Department S*, the name of a branch of Interpol featured in the '60s UK TV mystery series. Their speciaility was solving apparently unsolvable crimes. The show starred Peter Wyngarde as the foppish author/detective, Jason King.

Easybeats

The Easybeats were named after the BBC Light Radio pop program *Easybeat*, the name being suggested by their drummer Gordon Fleet.

Eve 6

Originally called Yakoo (until the somewhat surprising discovery of a Canadian band with that name), then Eleventeen (which was considered too youthful), this band was named after an episode of their favorite TV show, *The X-Files*, which featured female clones.

Flowerpot Men

The Flowerpot Men were named after an animated UK children's TV series popular in the 1960s, where the main characters, Bill and Ben, lived in a garden and were made entirely of flower pots.

Herman's Hermits

Lead singer Peter Noone was nicknamed Sherman from his likeness to the US cartoon character of that name in the '60s animated TV show, *The Rocky & Bullwinkle Show*. After a chance remark by a barman they adopted the backing group name Hermits, leading them to shorten "Sherman" to "Herman".

L7

"L7" is a term originating in the '50s meaning 'square' (i.e. put an L and a 7 together and you form a square), and was heard on *The Flintstones* cartoon series by guitarist Susie Gardner.

Living Colour

The name Living Colour comes from the old NBC TV announcement "The following program is brought to you in living color". Although they are a US band, they chose the English spelling of "colour" as it was thought to be more interesting (guitarist Vernon Reid had been born in London, but moved to Brooklyn as a child). Muzz Skillings (bass–*b.* Manuel Skillings).

Ned's Atomic Dustbin

"Ned's Atomic Dustbin" was the title of an episode of the UK comedy show *The Goons*, in which the character of Neddy Seagoon presents his plans for an anti-atomic dustbin (trashcan) to the British Prime Minister; the show was first broadcast on the radio in January 1959. A copy of the script was owned by vocalist Jonn Penney's mother and she would read it to him at bedtime.

Patti Page

Born Clara Ann Fowler, she joined the US TV show *Meet Patti Page*, sponsored by the Page Milk Company, and took the character name with her when she left.

Soup Dragons

The name of this band was taken from a character in the UK children's animated TV series *Clangers*, about the inhabitants of a remote planet. The Soup Dragon lived in a "soup well" and distributed soup to the hungry inhabitants of the planets, including Clangers.

Stooges

Originally named The Psychedelic Stooges, their name was inspired by the 1930s Columbia TV show, *The Three Stooges*, starring Jerome Lester Horwitz as "Curly", Moses Horwitz as "Moe" and Louis Feinberg as "Larry". The band later shortened the name to Stooges.

Swinging Blue Jeans

Starting out as The Bluegenes, they then obtained a slot on the UK TV show *Swingtime*, which was sponsored by a blue jeans company, so they extended (and slightly modified) their group name accordingly.

Talking Heads

"Talking Heads" came from a phrase seen in a TV guide, referring to a head-shot of someone talking directly into the camera.

Timelords

This name was taken from the UK BBC TV sci-fi series, *Doctor Who*. The Time Lords are a fictional race of humanoids from the planet Gallifrey, who have the ability to regenerate up to 12 times and who have also mastered time travel. The main character, Doctor Who, is a Time Lord.

Unit Four Plus Two

This group was originally formed as a folk group called Unit Four, after the '60s UK radio show *Pick Of The Pops*, hosted by Alan Freeman. The show was divided into four units; Unit 1 featured chart newcomers, Unit 2 premiered new releases, Unit 3 featured LPs, and Unit 4 ran down that week's Top-10 records. The group then added two more members when they branched into pop music, and extended their name to Unit Four Plus Two.

Young Rascals

This group were originally formed as The Rascals, before being re-named after the children's TV comedy *The Young Rascals*. On leaving their teens they reverted once again to being known as The Rascals.

Discography

Bands whose names were inspired
by songs and albums

a-ha

Band member Pål Waaktar had written a song called "a-ha", and the phrase was spotted by fellow band member Morten Harket as he leafed through Pål's notebook–Morten thought it would make a great name for a band. Once the group realized that the phrase was used internationally, they decided to use it as their band name. Pål Waaktaar (guitars, vocals–b. Pål Garnst) later adopted his mother's maiden name).

Alarm

The Alarm were originally a punk rock band called the Toilets, before changing their name to 17. While they were still known as 17, they wrote a song called "Alarm Alarm", later adapting the song title for their final name.

Kokomo Arnold

Born James Arnold, his stage name came from his hit "Kokomo Blues", Kokomo being a brand of coffee.

Aztec Camera

"Camera" came from the B-side of a **Teardrop Explodes'** single ("Sleeping Gas" c/w "Camera, Camera" c/w "Kirkby Workers Dream Fades", 1979), while "Aztec" was added because it was felt that it sounded right.

Badfinger

Badfinger, who were discovered by and recorded on The Beatles' record label Apple, took their name from "Badfinger Boogie", the working title for the Beatles song "With A Little Help From My Friends".

Bangles

The Bangles started out as the Supersonic Bangs, which came from a headline in Esquire magazine covering '60s hairstyles ("bangs" is used in the US to describe the fringe of hair on the forehead). Later they abbreviated the name to The Bangs, which was further modified to Bangles after the discovery of a similarly named band. The word "Bangles" came from a track ("Bangles") on the Electric Prunes album *The Electric Prunes* (1967).

Black Sabbath

The name Black Sabbath comes from a song written by bassist Geezer Butler (a fan of horror writer Denis Wheatley) about a scary vision he had, while with the Sabbath-forerunner Polka Tulk. The title of the song was inspired by a 1963 horror movie of the same name starring Boris Karloff and directed by Mario Bava. Lead guitarist Tony Iommi has been quoted as saying that the final name was picked "because we liked it", to try and alleviate the satanic links. The earlier name Polka Tulk has been variously remembered as a) "some famous war" according to guitarist Tony Iommi, b) having been seen by vocalist **Ozzy Osbourne** in his sister's bathroom on a tin of talcum powder (Polk Talc), or c) from a local Asian clothes shop. After Polka Tulk, they then changed to Earth, which was already being used by an existing pop group, so finally Black Sabbath was chosen.

Blue Rondo A La Turk

This comes from the name of a famous jazz song, recorded by Dave Brubeck in 1960 and itself based on "Rondo alla Turca" by Mozart.

Boxcar Willie

Boxcar Willie was born Lecil Travis Martin, his stage name being taken from the title of a song he wrote, "Boxcar Willie". He was driving in Lincoln, Nebraska and had stopped at a railroad crossing. While he was waiting for the train to go by, he saw a man sitting alone in a boxcar who looked just like his chief boom microphone operator, Willie Wilson. He pulled over to the side of the road immediately and wrote the song.

Butthole Surfers

The Butthole Surfers were known variously as the Ashtray Baby Heads and Nine Foot Worm Makes Home Food, eventually taking their more well-known name after a radio DJ mistook the name of one of their songs as being the name of the band.

Canned Heat

Canned Heat was taken from a 1928 song by bluesman Tommy Johnson, "Canned Heat Blues", and was chosen by vocalist Bob Hite.

Nick Cave & The Bad Seeds

Nick Cave's previous band, The Birthday Party had recorded an EP called *The Bad Seed* in 1983, so this name was chosen for his new band.

Cocteau Twins

The Cocteau Twins were named from a Simple Minds song originally called "The Cocteau Twins", but eventually appearing as "No Cure" on their first album, *Life In A Day*

(1989). In an earlier incarnation the band were backing Simple Minds and had seen the song on a set list. The original lyrics concern two gay friends who were into poet/movie director/novelist Jean Cocteau.

Cure

Originally named Easy Cure after one of their early numbers, the name was later shortened by Robert Smith to Cure as it sounded less hippy.

Curved Air

Originally formed as Sisyphus, they changed at the suggestion of Francis Monkman (keyboards), taking their new name from the title of a 1969 album recorded by Terry Riley, *A Rainbow In Curved Air*.

Deacon Blue

Deacon Blue is the name of a track on the album *Aja* by **Steely Dan**, although Ricky Ross denies Steely Dan were a particular influence–apparently he was walking down Tottenham Court Road in London, and thinking that Van Morrison had played the Dominion Theatre there, when the name popped into his head.

Deep Purple

This name was taken from the early '60s hit single "Deep Purple" by Nino Tempo and April Stevens, which happened to be the favorite song of guitarist Richie Blackmore's grandmother. This is probably just as well, as the other name they considered was Concrete God. Prior to that they were known as Roundabout, from a suggestion by early band member Chris Curtis.

Dixie Chicks

The name Dixie Chicks was inspired by "Dixie Chicken", the title track from the 1973 album of the same name by **Little Feat**, which came on the radio as they were driving to a show one day. The initial name was Dixie Chicken, then Chix, finally settling on Dixie Chicks.

Dr Feelgood

Johnny Kidd & the Pirates' guitarist Mick Green was one of guitarist Wilko Johnson's heroes, and this name was taken from a Johnny Kidd & the Pirates B-side "Doctor Feel-Good". That song was itself a cover of the hit by bluesman Piano Red, under the pseudonym Dr Feelgood & the Interns, which he used for his '60s comeback. Lee Brilleaux (vocals–b. Lee Collinson, re-named on account of his hair resembling a Brillo pad), Wilko Johnson (guitars–b. John Wilkinson), Sparko (bass–b. John Sparks), The Big Figure (drums–b. John Martin).

Fleetwood Mac

Contrary to popular belief, this name wasn't taken directly from the surnames of band members Mick Fleetwood and John McVie–it was actually from the title of an unreleased 1967 instrumental recorded by Fleetwood, McVie and Peter Green, during spare studio time while with John Mayall's Bluesbreakers.

Freddie & The Dreamers

Originally The Kingfishers, they were re-named The Dreamers when vocalist Freddie Garrity began to be featured. The name was inspired by the Johnny Burnette song "Dreamin'", a top–5 hit in the UK.

Golden Earring

Initially known as The Tornadoes, they were forced to change when the UK band of the same name had a #1 hit with "Telstar". The first choice was The Golden Earrings, taken from the song "Golden Earrings" by Peggy Lee, recorded in 1947.

Green Day

Originally named Sweet Children, they wrote the song "Green Day" about hanging out and smoking pot, later deciding to adopt the song title as their group name too. Billy Joe (vocals, guitars–*b.* Billie Joe Armstrong); Mike Dirnt (bass) was born Michael Pritchard and was given up for adoption; Tre Cool (drums–*b.* Frank Edwin Wright III) was re-named by punk vocalist Lawrence Livermore, on joining his band as drummer when only 12 years of age!

Groundhogs

. Originally called John Lee's Groundhogs, the name was taken from the John Lee Hooker song "Groundhog Blues", this being group leader Tony McPhee's favorite song of Hooker's.

Happy Mondays

The Happy Mondays took their name as a response to the profits made by Factory Records from label-mates **New Order's** single "Blue Monday".

Hothouse Flowers

Changing from their original name of The Benzini Brothers, *Hot House Flowers* came from the title of a 1984 album by jazz trumpeter Wynton Marsalis.

Icehouse

Originally named Flowers, their first album in 1981 was called *Icehouse*. They subsequently discovered that a band called Flowers already existed, so they re-named themselves Icehouse, and re-issued the first album as *Flowers*. Iva Davies (guitar, vocals–*b*. Ivor Davies).

Jo Jo Gunne

Band member Jay Ferguson was flipping through a music encyclopedia searching for inspiration for a name, and landed on one of his favorite artists, Chuck Berry. He decided to use one of Berry's songs, "Jo Jo Gunne", about a meddlesome monkey which causes a fight between a lion and an elephant, which the whole of the jungle comes to watch. The song is itself based on the African-American folk tale of "The Signifying Monkey", derived from a trickster figure of Yoruba (Nigerian) mythology.

Judas Priest

Judas Priest were named after a previous band of the same name, who in turn had taken their name from "The Ballad of Frankie Lee and Judas Priest" by **Bob Dylan** on the album *John Wesley Harding* (1967).

Madness

Madness started out as a ska band, and their name was inspired by the title of a 1963 song by ska artist Prince Buster. Suggs (*b*. Graham McPherson) took his nickname from a flautist in a jazz encyclopedia; Chas Smash (*b*. Cathal Joseph Patrick Smythe), used his teen alias as his stage name.

Mansun

Originally called Grey Lantern, this band took their new name from "A Man Called Sun" by The Verve, a single released in 1992 and featured on *The Verve EP*.

Matchbox

Matchbox took their name in tribute to a 1957 release by Carl Perkins, which was itself a reworking of Blind Lemon Jefferson's "Matchbox Blues", first recorded in 1927.

Matthews Southern Comfort

Matthews Southern Comfort was named after the title of leader and founder Ian Matthews' (*b.* Ian Matthews McDonald) solo album, recorded in 1970. Matthews had shortened his name to avoid confusion with King Crimson's sax player Ian McDonald.

McCoys

This name comes from a song called "The Real McCoy", which was named after a popular TV show of the time starring Walter Brennan, and was the B-side of the Ventures 1960 hit "Walk Don't Run".

Moody Blues

The Moody Blues were originally called the M & B Five, after the local brewery M & B (short for Mitchell's & Butlers) in England's Midlands district. They later chose the name Moody Blues to fit the original initials, which was taken from a Slim Harpo instrumental, "Moody Blues", on the album *Slim Harpo Sings Rainin' In My Heart* (1961).

Motorhead

"Motorhead" (an Americanism for a speed freak), the title of the B-side of the 1974 **Hawkwind** single "Kings of Speed", was the last song written by bassist Lemmie (b. Ian Frasier Kilminster) while with Hawkwind, prior to leaving to form Motorhead. Lemmie had initially wanted to call the band Bastard.

New Kids On The Block

Originally Nynuk, they were re-named New Kids On The Block by their record company after a song of the same name given to them by producer Maurice Starr, who had created the group as revenge against being fired by his previous band New Edition.

Nice

The Nice took their name from the **Small Faces'** song, "Here Comes The Nice", which is allegedly about amphetamines.

Robert Nighthawk

Born Robert McCollum, he took his mother's maiden name McCoy for a while, before taking his stage name from his 1937 song "Prowlin' Nighthawk".

Orchestral Manouevres in the Dark

Orchestral Manouvres in the Dark (AKA OMD) was taken from the title of a song idea thought up by band member Andy McCluskey while still at school. The name was chosen so that they wouldn't be mistaken for a punk band (they formed in 1978, at the height of the punk rock era). However, the song was never finished.

Pretenders

This name was inspired by Sam Cooke's version of The Platters hit "The Great Pretender", featured on the 1960 album *Hit's Of The '50s*. A skinhead known to Pretenders' lead vocalist Chrissie Hynde had shared with her that this was, somewhat surprisingly, his favorite song.

Pretty Things

The Pretty Things took their name from the **Bo Diddley** song "Pretty Thing", recorded in 1955. John Stax (bass–*b.* John Fullegar)

Psychedelic Furs

This name was inspired by "Venus in Furs", a track by the **Velvet Underground** on their first album *Velvet Underground and Nico* (1967).

Public Enemy

Taken from their early demo "Public Enemy #1", itself a term coined by FBI director J. Edgar Hoover. The name was adopted by Chuck D (*b.* Carlton Ridenour) as a condemnation of the general attitude towards young black men as being inherently criminal. Flavor Flav (*b.* William Drayton), Terminator X (*b.* Norman Rogers), Professor Griff (*b.* Richard Griffin).

Radiohead

Originally forming while still at school as On A Friday, that being the only day they could get to practise together, an early gig review prompted a change of name. The final choice of Radiohead came from a **Talking Heads** track "Radio Head" on *True Stories* (1986).

Rolling Stones

While generally considered to have been inspired by the **Muddy Waters** song "Rollin' Stone", the name actually comes from a line in another Muddy Waters song, "Mannish Boy", and was chosen by blues purist Brian Jones (guitars, b. Lewis Brian Hopkin Jones). The group was originally called Rollin' Stones, the "g" being added by their management. Bill Wyman (bass–b. Bill Perks) met someone called Gordon Lee Whyman while in the British Air Force, and decided he liked his last name and so later adopted it as his stage name (albeit with slightly different spelling). Mick Jagger & Keith Richard sometimes used the writing pseudonym Nanker/Phelge (also suggested by Brian Jones, and first used on "Stoned", the B-side of an early hit single "I Wanna Be Your Man"); "Phelge" came from an ex-roommate named James Phelge, and "Nanker" came from a term used by the band members to describe the act of making a revolting face.

Roxette

Dr Feelgood was one of Roxette guitarist Per Gessle's favorite bands, and "Roxette" was taken from a song on their album *Down By The Jetty* (1974). The name had been used by Gessle's previous band Gyllene Tider (Swedish for Golden Age or Golden Time) when they unsuccessfully tried to release an album in the States.

Selecter

"Selecter" was the title of a song written by group member Neol Davies called "The Selecter", a ska-style track which celebrated '60s Jamaican music. The 2-Tone record label had decided to use the song to back **The Specials'** single

"Gangsters", thereby leading Davies to put together a band and naming it after the song.

Sepultura

A Brazilian heavy-metal band, "sepultura" is Portuguese (the national language of Brazil) for "grave", and was chosen by founder Max Cavalera while translating the lyrics to the Motorhead song "Dancing On Your Grave".

Shakespear's Sister

This was inspired by a song of the same name by **The Smiths** (from the 1987 album *Louder Than Bombs*). Shakespeare was accidentally mis-spelt by the sleeve designer, so the group decided to keep it that way.

Sisters Of Mercy

"Sisters of Mercy" was the title of a Leonard Cohen song about prostitutes, on the 1968 album *Songs of Leonard Cohen*. Andrew Eldritch (*b*. Andrew William Harvey Taylor); Gary Marx (guitars–*b*. Mark Pairman) suggested the band name.

Spice Girls

The Spice Girls were a manufactured band originally intended by the management to be called Touch, until another band with that name surfaced. The name Spice Girls was inspired by a song entitled "Sugar and Spice", that had been written for them by Tim Hawes, a staff writer at London's Trinity Studios, where their early rehearsals were held. The initial suggestion (possibly by Hawes although Mel B also claims credit) was Spice, but the longer Spice Girls was eventually chosen. Individual names were bestowed on the group members by the UK teen music magazine, *Top of the Pops*. Scary *AKA* Mel B (*b.* Melanie Janine Brown), Baby (*b.* Emma Lee Burton), Posh (*b.* Victoria Adams), Ginger (*b.* Geri Estelle Halliwell), Sporty *AKA* Mel C (*b.* Melanie Jayne Chisholm).

Squeeze

Squeeze took their name from the name of the final **Velvet Underground** album, *Squeeze*, recorded in 1971. Squeeze's eponymous first album, released in 1978, was fittingly produced by ex-Velvet Underground member John Cale.

Steeleye Span

Folk guitarist Martin Carthy was a friend of the band, and he suggested this name while staying at group member Tim Hart's house one night. The name comes from a traditional Lincolnshire, UK folk song, "Harkstow Grange" (also known as "The Miser and his Man"), about a feud between two men called John Bowlin and Jon "Steeleye" Span.

Stiff Little Fingers

This name comes from the title of a song on The Vibrators debut album, *Pure Mania* (1977). Stiff Little Fingers were originally called The Fast, a reference to their musical style, however they had wanted to change and their promoter was pestering them for a permanent name. He called band member Jake Burns to discuss a new name, so Burns picked up the nearest album cover (which happened to be the Vibrators album) and read the name of one of the tracks–"Stiff Little Fingers". As with The Fast, it was expected that this name was for one gig only and would later be changed.

Stone Poneys

Stone Poneys were named after bluesman Charley Patton's song "Stone Poney Blues".

Strawberry Switchblade

This name comes from an obscure song title by the group Orange Juice, which is unavailable on record. Group members Jill Bryan and Rose McDowall had befriended Orange Juice's James Kirk, who suggested they form a band and also told them the name of a song he was writing–entitled "Strawberry Switchblade".

Suede

Suede are named after Morrissey's hit "Suedehead", which appeared on his album *Viva Hate* (1988). The band is known as London Suede in the US as a Washington DC-based folk singer, Suzanne DeBronkart, had previously recorded under the name Suede.

Toad The Wet Sprocket

Toad The Wet Sprocket got their name from an Eric Idle monologue called "Rock Notes" from the Monty Python album *Monty Python Contractual Obligation Album* (1980) . The monolog was a skit on music journalism and featured made-up bands including Toad the Wet Sprocket and The Dead Monkeys, as well as TV singing star Charisma. Idle had intended to use a name so stupid that no band would ever choose it! The group had intended to use the name for their first gig only, but decided to keep it. They later presented Idle with a platinum disc of their album *Dulcinea*, in gratitude for use of the name.

Kitty Wells

Born Muriel Ellen Deason, her stage name was chosen by her husband Johnnie Wright in 1943 from an old popular song, "Sweet Kitty Wells", originally recorded by the Pickard Family in 1930.

Youngbloods

The Youngbloods took their name from a solo album *Young Blood* (1965), released by leader Jesse Colin Young (*b.* Perry Miller). Young had been re-named by his producer Bobby Scott from a mixture of the names of Wild West outlaws Jesse James and Cole Younger, and Grand Prix racing driver Colin Chapman.

The Acknowledgements

Bands whose names were inspired
by other artists and groups

Beatles

The Beatles' name was suggested by John Lennon, taking inspiration from another band named after insects, **The Crickets**. The spelling was changed from Beetles to indicate their style of music at that time, i.e. Beat Music. UK TV company ITV's *Anthology* series suggested that the inspiration was a gang name in the movie *The Wild One* (1954), directed by Laslo Badenek and starring Marlon Brando and Lee Marvin.

Marc Bolan

Marc Bolan was born Marc Feld. He later changed his name at age 17 to Toby Tyler, when he first began performing on the folk circuit around the UK. Decca Records christened him Marc Bowland without his permission, indeed the first he knew of it was on receiving advance copies of his first recording, "The Wizard". After discussions with Decca, he shortened his last name to Bolan, a composite of the name of one of his heroes, **Bo(b) (Dy)lan**.

Chemical Brothers

Originally calling themselves The Dust Brothers, in tribute to the **Beastie Boys** production team of that name, they were ironically forced to change under threat of legal action by the original Dust Brothers. They considered using The Grit Brothers (suggested by band member Ed Simons's grandmother), before settling on Chemical Brothers. They had previously recorded the song "Chemical Beats" as The Dust Brothers.

Dr John

Born Malcolm John "Mac" Rebennack, Dr John used Henry Bird's stage alias **Professor Longhair** as inspiration for his own persona, Dr John the Night Tripper. The latter part of the name is a reference to **The Beatles'** hit single, "Day Tripper".

Chris Farlowe

Born John Henry Deighton, he took his stage name in honor of the US jazz guitarist Tal Farlowe, choosing the first name Chris because he particularly liked that name.

Guns N Roses

This name is a hybrid of the band members' previous group names, LA Guns and Hollywood Rose. Vocalist Axl Rose (*b.* Bill Bailey) took his stage name from his natural father William Rose and his band at the time, Axl– although the name Axl Rose is much touted as being an anagram of Oral Sex, this was not the inspiration. Guitarist Slash (*b.* Saul Hudson) was named for his playing style. Izzy Stradlin (guitars–*b.* Jeffrey Isbell), Duff McCagan (bass–*b.* Michael McCagan).

Howlin' Wolf

Born Chester Arthur Burnett (named for Chester Arthur, the 21st president of the United States), he first began using the stage name "Howlin' Wolf" when he was a DJ with Arkansas radio station KWEM, taking the name from the 1930s release "The Original Howling Wolf", by John "Funny Papa" Smith.

Ladysmith Black Mambazo

The members of this group were mainly from the township of Ladysmith in South Africa. They took their name from the Zulu word for axe, which is "mambazo", as a tribute to the Black Mambazo choral group which was active in South Africa in the 1950s.

Martha & The Vandellas

Originally called the Del-Phi's, leader Martha Reeves was ordered to come up with a replacement name by Motown boss Berry Gordy, under threat of being re-named The Tillies. Using the beginning of the Del-Phi's name, and also Della Reese, who was already a star and whom Reeves had recently seen singing at a church in Detroit, she came up with "della", then added the prefix "Van" from Van Dyke Street in Detroit, where her grandmother lived. Reeves had earlier used the name Martha Lavaille, which had been suggested by her Aunt Berniece.

Monkees

The Monkees were one of the first manufactured bands, being brought together by NBC TV in the States, and the name was based on the Beatles, i.e. a mis-spelt animal name. Other names which were considered included The Inevitables and The Turtles. **The Beatles'** connection was further extended by the format of their show, which was based on the Beatles' movie *A Hard Day's Night* (1964), also they acquired the nickname "Pre-Fab Four" in reference to the Beatles' nickname of "Fab Four" and the fact that they were a "pre-fabricated" boy band. The show was re-created in the 1980s with four new actors, calling themselves The New Monkees. Peter Tork formed a band, also in the 1980s, which he christened The New Monks. Peter Tork (bass–*b*. Peter Thorkelson).

Matt Monro

Matt Monro was born Terry Parsons. The last part of his stage name was suggested by pianist Winifred Atwell (who had recommended him to Decca Records), "Monro" being her father's name. "Matt" was taken from a journalist friend of his, named Matt White.

Mötley Crüe

This name was taken from that of a defunct '70s band, Mottley Croo. The band used umlauts in tribute to Löwenbräu beer, and not as a Nazi reference as is often reported. Bandmembers Vince Neil (*b*. Vincent Neil Wharton); Tommy Lee (*b*. Tommy Lee Bass). Mick Mars (*b*. Robert "Bob" Alan Deal) changed his name because he didn't like the initials associated with Bob Alan Deal (B.A.D.), picking "Mick" because he had always liked that name, and "Mars" from the Roman God of War. Nicki Sixx (*b*. Frank Carlton Serafino Ferrano) changed his name legally after being rejected by his father (also called Frank Ferrano), and took the name Nikki Sixx after his friend Angie's ex-boyfriend Niki Syxx. He later told journalists that the name was based on the fist two digits of his California drivers license, N6.

Pink Floyd

Pink Floyd were named by original member **Syd Barrett**, initially as The Pink Floyd Sound, after Carolina bluesmen Pink Anderson and Floyd Council. Earlier names had included Sigma 6, The T-Sets, The Abdabs, The Screaming Abdabs, The Architectural Abdabs (Roger Waters had attended architectural college), Sigma 6 (again), before changing to The Pink Floyd Sound after Barrett joined.

Ramones

The name Ramones was inspired by the pseudonym, Paul Ramon, used by Paul McCartney for production purposes in the '60s. The various band members adopted the surname Ramone to suggest brotherly togetherness. Joey Ramone (b. Jeffrey Hyman), Johnny Ramone (b. John Cummings), Dee Dee Ramone (b. Douglas Colvin), Tommy Ramone (b. Thomas Erdelyi).

Red Hot Chili Peppers

Red Hot Chili Peppers took their name from a combination of two early jazz and blues band names–jazz trumpeter Louis Armstrong's The Hot Five, and Jelly Roll Morton's Red Hot Peppers. The name was suggested by band member Flea (b. Michael Peter Balzary) who himself had learned to play jazz trumpet and idolized Louis Armstrong. Balzary became known as "Mike B The Flea" while at high school, which eventually got shortened to "Flea".

Roman Holliday

"Roman holiday" is slang for a good time, while the double 'L' in 'Holliday' was in honor of blues singer **Billie Holiday**, although, unfortunately, they used an incorrect spelling of her name.

Sneaker Pimps

Originally called Line of Flight, the Sneaker Pimps took their name after watching an interview with the **Beastie Boys** on the UK TV Channel 4 music show, The Word. When asked about their interesting sneakers, Beastie Boys'

Mike D said that they had a guy who searched out classic trainers for them, and referred to him as a "sneaker pimp". The Beastie Boys have since denied ever using the term.

Sonic Youth

This name was taken from two sources:- Fred "Sonic" Smith, guitarist with the **MC5** and husband to Patti Smith, and Big Youth, the '70s dub reggae star. Band member Thurston Moore has said the name came to him in a dream when he was aged 17.

Stone Roses

Originally named English Rose, they later changed their name to include a reference to their favorite band, the **Rolling Stones**. Mani (bass–b. Gary Mountfield), Reni (drums–b. Alan Wren).

Ugly Kid Joe

Opening one night for Pretty Boy Floyd, an LA glam-rock band, they were about to go on and still didn't have a name, so chose a joke version of Pretty Boy Floyd's name with the intention of changing it later.

Rudy Vallee

Rudy Vallee was born Hubert Prior Vallee, taking the name Rudy because of his admiration for saxophonist Rudy Weidoft.

Yardbirds

Singer Keith Relf was intrigued by the fact that writer Jack Kerouac kept referring to jazz sax player Charlie Parker in his works. On investigating further, Relf discovered that

Parker's nickname was "Bird", short for "Yardbird", which is slang for a railroad hobo, and decided to use that as the band's name.

ZZ Top

The name ZZ Top was inspired by a combination of a poster of Texas bluesman Z. Z. Hill, together with "Zig Zag" and "Top" cigarette rolling papers.

Music Industrial

Bands and artists whose names were inspired
by non-performing aspects of music

Altered Images

This name refers to a sleeve design on **The Buzzcocks'** single "Promises", and was inspired by The Buzzcocks vocalist, Pete Shelley's constant interfering with the initial sleeve designs.

Erykah Badu

Born Erykah Wright, her alter-ego "badu" comes from a phrase she used to repeat while jazz scat-singing. It was later discovered that the word meant "manifesting truth and light" in Arabic.

Bow Wow Wow

Bow Wow Wow were named by Malcolm McLaren when the ex-members of **Adam Ant's** backing band asked him for help in forming a new band. The name was inspired by the famous HMV (His Master's Voice) record label, whose logo shows a dog sitting next to an old-fashioned gramophone. Anabelle Lwin (vocals–b. Myant Myant Aye Dunn-Lwin) was also re-named by McLaren. The group also at one time included in its line-up **Boy George**, known then as Lieutenant Lush.

Eurythmics

While at school, band member Annie Lennox had been taught a dance form (actually called "eurhythmics") by teacher Marguerite Feltges. Eurhythmics had been developed by Emile Jacques-Dalcroze in 1903 to teach children music through movement, and was based on Greek dance.

Hooters

During the recording of their first demo, the band were loaned a Hohner Melodica, a type of keyboard harmonica referred to by musicians as a hooter. The recording engineer at this session, John Senior, kept demanding "more hooter" (shades of Christopher Walken hankering for more cowbell as **Blue Oyster Cult**'s record producer on *Saturday Night Live*), and the name stuck.

Jam

The Jam was shortened from the phrase "Lunchtime Jam", used when the band would practice during school lunch breaks. Paul Weller (vocals, guitars–b. John William Weller) changed his name in honor of Paul McCartney.

Tommy James & The Shondells

Thomas Gregory Jackson chose the stage name Tommy James on signing with Roulette Records in 1966. The label had asked him if he wanted to change his name, as they were going to bring him to the forefront of the Shondells (already famous with the hit song "Hanky Panky"), so he decided to take a single-syllable name but keeping the initial letter "J". "Shondell" was a word he had made up in high school, that he thought sounded like a music term.

NRBQ

Members of the band The Seven Of Us became a quintet on signing a new drummer, and began using a couple of alternative names, New Rockabilly Quintet and New Rhythm & Blues Quintet. After Columbia Records dropped them, vocalist Frank Gadler quit so they became the New Rhythm & Blues Quartet, later abbreviated to the final name of NRBQ.

Planxty

Originally named CLAD, from the initial letters of the members' names (Christy Moore, Liam O'Flynn, Andy

Irvine, Donal Lunny), they later adopted the name Planxty, which is an Irish word for a song written in tribute to someone.

Specials AKA

Specials AKA formed as a ska band in Coventry, UK as The Coventry Specials, with Specials being taken from the "special" one-shot records made for the early Jamaican sound systems. The name was later changed to Specials AKA.

Sugarhill Gang

The Sugarhill record label was formed by R'n'B singer Sylvia Robinson in 1979, Sugar Hill being a section of New York's Harlem district. "Rapper's Delight" was released on her label by an unknown group of rappers which she christened The Sugarhill Gang, after the record label.

Yazoo

Vince Clarke, who had recently left **Depeche Mode**, answered an ad in the UK music magazine Melody Maker which had been placed by Alison Moyet, asking for "rootsy blues musicians". The name Yazoo was taken from the name of the American blues label, itself named for Yazoo City, Mississippi.

Artistic License

Bands whose names were
inspired by the Arts

Adam & The Ants

Adam Ant, *b.* Stuart Leslie Goddard, took the name Adam from his love of a painting of the Garden of Eden. He chose the name Ants for the backing group because groups with insect names had traditionally done well (e.g. **Beatles**, **Crickets**) and also because the insect's work ethic appealed to him. He often changed stage names betweeen gigs, using at one time the pseudonym Eddie Riff. Mark Gaumont (guitars–*b.* Mark Ryan); Dave Barbarossa (drums–*b.* Dave Barbe); Merrick (drums–*b.* Chris Hughes).

Amen Corner

The group took its name from the title of a play by James Baldwin, concerning a Harlem family with close ties to the local church. The term itself applies to the section of southern US churches where women would sit and periodically call out "Amen" during the sermon.

Arcadia

This was taken from a painting by Nicholas Poussin called "Arcadian Shepherds"–the inscription on the tomb around which the shepherds are gathered reads "ET IN ARCADIA EGO" ("Even in Arcadia I Exist"); Nick Rhodes had seen the painting and liked it.

Darling Buds

Band member Harley Farr (*b.* Gerraitt Farr, and nicknamed "Harley Davidson" because his dad had once been a Hell's Angel) was browsing his parents' bookshelf, looking for inspiration for a band name. He came across a copy of the novel *The Darling Buds of May* by H. E. Bates, which title was in turn taken from William Shakespeare's

Sonnet #18 ("...Rough winds do shake the darling buds of May...").

Divine Comedy

This group originally started out as a trio, then afterwards the name was used as an alias for group member Neil Hannon when he went solo. The name was inspired by Dante Alighieri's epic poem *The Divine Comedy*, published just before his death in 1321, a copy of which was seen on the Hannon family bookshelf.

Doors

Singer Jim Morrison was inspired by Aldous Huxley's *The Doors of Perception*, detailing a mescaline experience. Huxley's title was itself inspired by a line from *The Marriage Of Heaven And Hell*, a poem by William Blake –"If the doors of perception were cleansed, every thing would appear to man...as it is, infinite".

Hole

The name of this band was taken by Courtney Love from the line "There's a hole burning deep inside me" in Euripides' play *Medea*. Additionally, she has said that after complaining to her mother about her unsettled childhood, her mother told her not to walk around with a big hole inside herself. Courtney Love (vocals, guitars–*b*. Love Michelle Harrison) was re-christened Courtney Michelle Harrison after her parents split, later combining her two names for the stage.

Oingo Boingo

Oingo Boingo started out initially as a musical troupe affiliated with a movie production company formed in

Paris by Richard Elfman, brother of Oingo Boingo's leader Danny Elfman. The musical troupe was called "The Mystical Knights of Oingo Boingo", which was later shortened to Oingo Boingo.

Pere Ubu

Pere Ubu is the name of the central figure in the Alfred Jarry play *Ubu Roi*. The name was chosen because the band thought it both looked and sounded interesting, and because Jarry's plays involved the imagination of the audience in the scene-setting.

Soundgarden

Formed in Seattle, they took their name from *A Sound Garden*, which is the title of a hollow pipe sculpture in Sand Point Park, by the side of Seattle's Lake Washington. The sculpture produces musical tones when the wind blows through it. The band thought the name conjured up strong visual images.

Ooh, La La!

Bands whose names were
inspired by risqué themes

10 c.c.

10 c.c. were named by record producer Jonathan King, the original story being that it was inspired by the amount of semen in the average male ejaculation (i.e. 9 cc), with one cc added as they were better than average. In fact, the average male ejaculation contains only 3-5 cc of semen. This story has since been denied by King, who said that in fact the name came to him in a dream. The group started out as Hotlegs and had a UK top 10 hit with "Neanderthal Man" under that name.

Carter USM

Carter the Unstoppable Sex Machine (later shortened to USM), was a reference to guitarist Fruitbat's (b. Les Carter) energetic social life at the time. Fruitbat was a teenage nickname which he had adopted when joining a UK punk band called The Dead Clergy. Jim Bob (vocals–b. James Robert Morrison).

Extreme

The band have been quoted as saying that their name was intended to reflect their wide range of influences, although the local story at their inception suggests the name is a corruption of "X-Dream", as in X-rated dream.

Fanny

An all-girl rock group, the name Fanny was suggested by ex-Beatle George Harrison. Presumably it didn't create quite the stir in the States as it did in Britain, where the word is frequently used for a different part of the female anatomy.

Foetus

Born Jim Thirlwell, *AKA* Jim Foetus (Scraping Foetus Off The Wheel, You've Got Foetus On Your Breath, etc.), "Foetus" is used as a sort of generic name for the artist, who changes his stage name quite frequently. He has also used Clint Ruin and Manorexia as stage names.

Hot Tuna

Stories abound that they originally adopted the name Hot Shit, and were made to change for purposes of commercial acceptability. However, this has been consistently denied by the band. Guitarist Jorma Kaukonen has been quoted as saying that the name is an answer to a question posed in their song "Keep On Truckin'" (*Burgers*, 1972), as adapted from Blind Boy Fuller's 1938 song "What's That Smell Like Fish?". The answer, of course, is Hot Tuna.

Korn

Vocalist Jonathan Davis' had been at a party in his home town of Bakersfield, CA when he overheard two gay friends discussing a particularly distasteful incident during a recent sex session. When Jon passed the story on to friends he would later say "corn" to remind them of it and gross them out. The "R" in Korn is reversed, along with mixed upper and lower case letters, to represent a young child's scrawled handwriting. Brian "Head" Welch is so-called because he has a large head. Reggie Arvizu is nicknamed "Fieldy"–it started out at school as "Gopher" from his chubby cheeks, which was shortened to "Gar", this was then extended again to "Garfield", and finally "Fieldy". Jonathan Davis is nicknamed "HIV" as an ironic reference to the teasing he received at school by kids who mistakenly thought he was gay.

Lovin' Spoonful

"Lovin' Spoonful" was a term used in Mississippi John Hurt's "Coffee Blues", as a colloquialism for the male ejaculation, although at the time the band first came to prominence it was assumed to be a reference to drugs. The name was suggested to founder member John Sebastian by fellow musician and future collaborator Fritz Richmond, after Sebastian told him there were elements of Hurt's blues in their sound.

Jelly Roll Morton

Born Ferdinand Joseph Lemott (also spelled Lamothe in some references), "jelly roll" is a term used in blues vernacular to describe the penis. Morton acquired his nickname while touring the vaudeville circuit.

Pogues

The name Pogues was shortened from the original "Pogue Mo Chone", which is Gaelic for "kiss my arse", after a DJ at BBC Radio Scotland pointed out the meaning, resulting in them being banned from the BBC airwaves and forcing a change.

Steely Dan

The name Steely Dan was inspired by a steam-powered dildo which appeared in three iterations in William Burroughs' *The Naked Lunch*. Founder members Walter Becker and Donald Fagen were both keen readers of 1950s "Beat" literature, such as that written by Burroughs, and chose the name for a laugh, not expecting the group to last as long as it did.

Stone Temple Pilots

Stone Temple Pilots were originally called *Mighty Joe Young*, from the 1949 horror movie of the same name (subsequently re-made by Disney), but were forced to change by a Chicago bluesman who was using that name. Next, they took inspiration from the STP oil stickers which adorned their bikes. Early suggestions to go with the initials included Shirley Temple's Pussy and Stinky Toilet Paper, both of which were rejected by Atlantic Records, so the band settled on Stone Temple Pilots, which has no real meaning but fits the chosen initials.

Throbbing Gristle

"Throbbing gristle" is local (Yorkshire, England) slang for the male erection, and was chosen by the band to make people uncomfortable when asking their records. Cosey Fanni Tutti (*b.* Christine Carol Newby) hated her first name Christine, so first changed it to Cosmosis, and then shortened that to Cosey. Artist Robin Klassnik suggested she adopt the longer name Cosey Fanni Tutti, after the Mozart opera *Cosi Fan Tutte*. Genesis P-Orridge (*b.* Neil Andrew Megson).

Tower Of Power

Formed in Detroit and originally named The Motowns from their love of soul music, their new name was a term used colloquially for the male genitals, and was chosen as it was felt they had more chance of success with that name than the original name.

Velvet Underground

This name was taken from the title of a pornographic paperback which had been found in the subway. The book, *The Velvet Underground*, a novel about sado-masochism, was penned in 1963 by Michael Leigh.

W.A.S.P.

The group chose this acronym as it can represent different things to different people: White Anglo-Saxon Protestants, or the insect itself. It was initially thought to stand for We Are Sexual Perverts, as this was inscribed on their first record. Blackie Lawless is usually stated as having been born Stephen Duran, however he has said that his real name is Stephen Lawless and that "Blackie" was a teenage nickname.

Frank Zappa & Mothers Of Invention

Zappa was born *Frank* Vincent Zappa, not *Francis* as has been widely reported. The band was originally named The Mothers (as in the abbreviation of "motherfucker", a name which was conceived on Mother's Day), but the "of Invention" part (as in "Necessity is the Mother of Invention") was later nervously added by his record label, Bizarre Records.

Take The Stand

Bands whose names were inspired by legal
issues or which make a statement

311

A friend of the band was arrested for indecent exposure when caught skinny-dipping and was taken home by the police, naked and handcuffed, to his parents. The band thought this funny, and learning that the Omaha police code for indecent exposure is a "311", they decided to adopt as the band name. The rumor that the name refers to the KKK (as in Ku Klux Klan), with K being the 11th letter of the alphabet (i.e. 3x11), was strongly denied by the band as an unfortunate coincidence. P-Nut (*b.* Aaron Charles Wills, bass) got his nickname from someone saying that his head was like a peanut. SA Martinez (*b.* Douglas Vincent Martinez, rapper) was re-christened by vocalist Nick Hexum as SA on Hexum's return to Nebraska from California–SA stands for "Spooky Apparition", but also refers to the use of "ese" (like "dude", and pronounced "es-say") in everyday Hispanic parlance.

4 Non-Blondes

The name is not related to the fact that none of the band members is blonde; they were sitting in a San Francisco park eating pizza when a clean-cut family walked by. The little boy wanted to take some pizza to feed the birds with, but the parents admonished him, looking disapprovingly at the band. As the family were all blonde, the band decided to ironically name themselves 4 Non-Blondes.

999

999 were initially known as The Dials, then changed to 48 Hours, but this was dropped after **The Clash** recorded a song called "48 Hours". They finally settled on 999, which was the number for the UK emergency services, equivalent to 911 in the US.

Breeders

"Breeders" is a derogatory term used by homosexuals to describe straight people. Founder member Kim Deal had heard the term and thought it was funny, having previously used it as a band name when she and her sister Karen had played in and around Dayton, Ohio.

C.C.S.

C.C.S. was a 20-plus member band started by noted British blues player Alexis Korner (b. Alexis Koerner, he changed the spelling of his last name), after the UK musician's union had denied his previous band, The New Church, playing permits in the UK because one of the members was a Danish citizen. C.C.S. stands for Collective Consciousness Society, however in a radio interview Korner once joked it stood for Chigwell Co-operative Society, only to be corrected shortly after by a serious caller pointing out that it should be Chigwell AND DISTRICT Co-operative Society (Chigwell is a staid suburban village outside London).

Culture Club

This name developed from the original suggestion of Caravan Club. Vocalist **Boy George** later claimed that the name was derived from the fact that the band represented a mixture of cultures. The band started life as In Praise of Lemmings and changed to Sex Gang Children, before finally settling on Culture Club.

D.O.A.

Previously called The Skulls, they changed their name in 1978 to D.O.A., a medical term meaning Dead On Arrival. D.O.A. is now used as a pseudonym by original band member Joe Keighley (AKA Joey Shithead).

Devo

Devo were originally formed as the De-Evolution Band, a name inspired by their own theory of de-evolution, i.e. their belief that humans are in fact regressing rather than evolving. The theory was based on a book called *The Beginning Was The End: Knowledge Can Be Eaten*, by Oskar Kiss Maerth, which proposed that mankind has evolved from a strain of brain-eating apes.

Fugees

Fugees is short for "refugees", as used derogatorily to describe displaced Haitians–Wyclef Jean (*b.* Jeannel Wyclef Jean) having previously emigrated from Haiti. They were originally called Tranzlator Crew, but changed at the request of an existing new wave group, Translator. Pras Michel (*b.* Prakazrel Michel).

GBH

GBH stands for Grievous Bodily Harm, and is a legal term used in the UK to denote a certain level of wounding. They changed their name at one point to Charged GBH on the discovery of another band called GBH, but later reverted to GBH when the other group disbanded.

Jamiroquai

Jamiroquai was born Jason Kay (*AKA* Jay Kay), his stage name being a hybrid of "jam" (a term used for an impromptu music session) and "Iroquois", a North American Indian tribe. He had seen "Iroquois" on an American helicopter, the Bell 1H1V Iroquois, which had encouraged him to learn more about the Iroquois nation, after which he became inspired by their reverence for natural law and the good of the earth.

KLF

KLF started out as being an abbreviation for Kopyright Liberation Front, which was used on their early releases. Spelling copyright with a "k" is common practice in cases where in fact no copyright exists. Over time, the band proceeded to ascribe different meanings to the initials when interviewed. Bill Drummond (*b.* William Butterworth).

Living In A Box

"Living In A Box" was the title of a song written by Marcus Vere (keyboards) and Anthony Critchlow (drums), which they were recording at the same time as they were auditioning singers for their band. One of the singers (Richard Darbyshire) joined the band and they took the song title (a reference to the homeless of Britain during the lengthy term of Prime Minister Margaret Thatcher) as the band name.

New Order

New Order were formed out of the remains of **Joy Division** following vocalist Ian Curtis's suicide. Band member Rob Gretton had seen an article in the British newspaper *The Guardian*, which mentioned the People's New Oder of Kampuchea, and the phrase "New Order" caught his eye. Incidentally, the name New Order had previously been used by a mid-'70s LA-based band.

New Radicals

Although he had made two solo albums, founder member Gregg Alexander (*b.* Gregg Aiuto) decided to form a band, which he named New Radicals, a term that reflected his oppositional view of corporate America.

NWA

Band member Easy-E had set up a record label named Ruthless Records, for which future NWA members Ice Cube and **Dr Dre** were writing songs. They had offered "Boyz N The Hood" to one of Ruthless Records' bands, HBO, however HBO turned it down. Easy-E therefore decided to form a band with Ice Cube and Dr Dre in order to release the record, naming the band NWA, which is short for Niggaz With Attitude. Easy-E (*b.* Eric Wright); Ice Cube (*b.* O'Shea Jackson); MC Ren (*b.* Lorenzo Patterson); DJ Yella (*b.* Antoine Carraby); Dr Dre–see separate entry.

PIL

Initially formed as The Carnivorous Buttock Flies, the name Public Image Limited (later abbreviated to PIL) was used for the release of their first single, "Public Image", and was chosen to give the impression of a company rather than a rock band, that is, no managers, no producers, etc. Jah Wobble (bass–*b.* John Wardle).

Shadows

Originally named the Drifters, they were forced to change as the US group of that name would not allow them to appear in the States. The name Shadows was suggested by bass player Jet Harris, who felt that they were in the shadow of singer Cliff Richard. Harris (*b.* Terence Harris) acquired the nickname "Jet" at school for being a fast runner; Bruce Welch (bass–*b.* Bruce Cripps) changed to his mother's maiden name as that fit the pop star image better; Hank Marvin (guitars–*b.* Brian Robson Rankin) acquired the nickname "Hank" at school due to his bowlegged appearance, which made him walk like a cowboy. He originally called himself Hank B. Marvin, the initial "B" referring to his original name of "Brian"; Tony Meehan (*b.* Daniel Meehan).

That Petrol Emotion

This band were formed in Derry, Ireland and took their name from the lyrics of a song by another Derry-based band, Bam Bam and the Calling. The phrase is intended to represent the feelings associated with living in Northern Ireland during The Troubles.

Trammps

Starting out as The Volcanos and then being known as The Moods, The Trammps named themselves ironically in reference to a comment aimed at them to the effect that they would never amount to anything more than tramps.

Wailers

The Wailers started life as The Teenagers, then first changed their name to The Wailin' Rudeboys before becoming The Wailin' Wailers. Finally, the name was shortened to The Wailers. The term "wailers" referred to the hardships from living in Kingston ghettoes like Trench Town. Bunny Wailer was born Neville O'Reilly Livingston; Peter Tosh was born Peter McIntosh.

War

The L.A.-based Latin funk band Night Shift was joined by vocalist Eric Burdon at the suggestion of his managers, Steve Gold and Jerry Goldstein. At this point they changed their name to War, a shortened version of the original suggestion, War Is Music. The name was deliberately chosen to oppose the late '60s peace movement.

Re Issues

Bands whose names were inspired
by contemporary themes

5th Dimension

Originally The Versatiles, in reference to their varied musical backgrounds (R'n'B, gospel, soul, jazz, blues and opera), the band's name was later changed to The 5th Dimension to sound a little more modern, having been suggested by **Johnny Rivers** on signing them to his newly-formed Soul City Records.

B-52s

This band was formed in Athens, Georgia, and "B-52" is southern US slang for the type of bouffant hairstyle which the female members of the group wear, the hairstyle itself being named after a type of American warplane. They were billed as the "B.C.52s" when releasing the theme song to the movie *The Flintstones* (1994), directed by Brian Levant and starring John Goodman.

Crew Cuts

Originally called The Four Tones, the new name was suggested by Cleveland radio station WERE-AM DJ Bill Randle, in reference to their close-cropped hairstyles.

Funkadelic

"Funkadelic" was a term invented by founder/leader George Clinton to describe his band's sound, being a combination of "funk" and "psychedelic". The name change was necessary after he lost the rights to use his previous band name, **Parliament**.

Go-Go's

The Go-Go's were originally called The Misfits, then changed their name after several gigs around LA's punk club scene. The new name was thought up by group member Jane Weidlin while the band were eating in a Denny's restaurant on Sunset Boulevard in Los Angeles.

Kinks

This name was suggested by the group's manager Robert Wace after the fashionable '60s expression, "kinky", meaning outrageous or unusual. They were originally known as The Ravens, in homage to the Vincent Price film *The Raven* (1963), directed by Roger Corman.

Marcels

Group member Frederick Johnson had a hairstyle known as the Marcel French Finger Wave, and this provided the inspiration for the group's name.

Matchbox 20

Paul Doucette, the group's drummer, used to be a waiter. One day, somebody walked into the restaurant where he worked, wearing a shirt with the number 20 on it, covered in patches. The only one he could make out said "matchbox". He thought "Matchbox 20" sounded cool together and would make an excellent name for a line of clothing, so he later suggested the name for the band.

Merton Parkas

The Merton Parkas were a Mod group from Merton in South London, a "parka" being a type of coat favored by Mods. "Mod" was a term used by well-dressed British youths in the 1960s.

Small Faces

This name was suggested by a friend of Steve Marriott's called Annabelle. "Face" was a term used by the Mods of the 60's to describe someone who was a fashion trendsetter, and "Small" came from the fact that the group members were all quite short. The band later became known as The Faces.

Split Enz

The band originally formed with the name Split Ends, from the hairdressing term, but later changed to Split Enz. At the same time, the band members decided to go by their middle names rather than their first names, hence Tim Finn (*b.* Brian Timothy Finn), Noel Crombie (*b.* Geoffrey Noel Crombie), Emlyn Crowther (*b.* Paul Emlyn Crowther), Eddie Rayner (*b.* Anthony Edward Rayner), and Mike Chunn (*b.* Jonathan Michael Chunn). The one exception was Phil Judd (*b.* Phillip Raymond Judd), who remained as Phil.

Status Quo

Status Quo took their name from an Italian fashion shoe of the early '60s. Rick Parfitt is usually referenced as having been born Richard Harrison, however he was actually born Richard Parfitt. The confusion arises because early in his career he played in a group called The Highlights with twin sisters Gloria and Jean Harrison, so he adopted the stage name Ricky Harrison to give the impression of a family group.

Voice Of The Beehive

The band originally claimed that their name was taken from the title of a Bette Davis movie, but that wasn't the case, as no such movie title exists–actually it was inspired by their own beehive hairdos.

A Higher Plane

Bands whose names were inspired by
spiritual issues and coincidences

49ers

Dawn Mitchell, eventually chosen as the singer, was the 49th in line to be auditioned and this provided the inspiration for the name. There is no connection with the NFL football team, the San Francisco 49ers, or with the California Gold Rush of 1849.

Air Supply

This name came from a dream which band member Graham Russell had, in which he saw the words "AIR SUPPLY" in lights on a giant billboard.

Earth, Wind & Fire

Originally known as The Salty Peppers, the new name was taken from the three elements in vocalist Maurice White's astrological chart (White is a Sagittarian), substituting "wind" for "air" as it sounded better.

Enigma

"Enigma" is the Greek word for "'mystery", and was chosen by creator Michael Cretu, the creator of the group, because he wanted to make music steeped in mysticism. Cretu furthered the mystery by adopting the pseudonym Curly MC on the release of their 1990 single "Sadeness".

Jesus Loves You

This was a recording alias of **Boy George** and was chosen to pay tribute to the religious faith which had helped him through his drug addiction.

King Crimson

The name King Crimson is often referenced as being attributed to the Devil, like Satan or Beelzebub. However, group member Pete Sinfield, who suggested the name, has denied this and says that it was taken from a track on their first album, *In The Court Of The Crimson King* (1969), when they were under pressure to pick a name quickly.

Kula Shaker

Kula Shaker, who were at the time known as The Kays, were named in honor of a guy they had met who had changed his own name to Kula Sekhara, after a 9th-century Indian emperor and mystic. The guy told the band that, if they adopted the name, the original Kula Sekhara would watch over them.

Love

Love were forced to change from their original name after the similarly-named Grass Roots had a hit single. Group leader Arthur Lee chose the new name as he thought "love" was the best part of life. Lee was born Arthur Taylor Porter, but changed to Lee, the name of his mother's second husband, after his parents divorced.

Marshall Tucker Band

The band took their name from a key ring found on the floor of their rehearsal room, on which was inscribed the name "Marshall Tucker", actually later discovered to be the name of a piano tuner, and not the name of the owner of the rehearsal room as is commonly reported.

Nirvana

"Nirvana" is a Hindu word meaning "beatific state", the highest state of consciousness reached through meditation. The name was suggested by Kurt Cobain, who wanted a beautiful name rather than a hard, punk rock name. Chris Novoselic (*b.* Krist Novoselic).

PM Dawn

PM Dawn were named in reference to the well-known axiom "From the darkest hour comes the light". Group member Atrell Cordes goes by the aliases Prince Be, Reasons and The Nocturnal; Jarrett Cordes is also known as DJ Minutemix, JC and The Eternal.

Quicksilver Messenger Service

This name had a somewhat long-winded development process started by band member David Freiberg. The band members included four Virgos and a Gemini, both of which signs are ruled by the planet Mercury. In ancient times, Mercury the element was known as "Quicksilver". Mercury was also the name of the winged messenger of the gods, and Virgo was the servant–all of the above combined to become Quicksilver Messenger Service. Dino Valente (also spelled Valenti) was born Chester William Powers, Jr., and changed his name at 17–he continued to use his given name for songwriting credits, along with the pseudonym Jessi Oris Farrow.

Early Impressions

Bands and artists whose names were inspired
by issues from childhood and school

Alice In Chains

The name Alice In Chains is based on a name used by a band which vocalist Layne Staley had previously fronted while in high school. The original incarnation was named "Alice N Chains", a cross-dressing glam-rock band who had originally formed with the name Sleze.

Alisha's Attic

Alisha is a fictional character created by group members Shellie and Karen Poole (daughters of Brian Poole, leader of the '60's pop band The Tremeloes). The character is based on an imaginary childhood friend whom Shellie, who suffered from Obsessive-Compulsive Disorder, communicated with between the ages of 4 and 13. "Attic" comes from the attic studio belonging to a composer friend, Terry Martin, where they originally recorded demos.

Anthrax

Anthrax is an infectious disease found in grazing animals, such as cattle and sheep, which is transmissible to people. Guitarist Scott Ian (b. Scott Ian Rosenfeld) got the name from a high school biology class, thinking the name sounded good for a heavy metal band. The band came under pressure to change their name after the anthrax attacks following the events of September 11, 2001, but did not do so. Joey Belladonna (vocals–b. Joseph Belladini).

Babes In Toyland

Babes In Toyland was the name of a 1934 movie starring Laurel and Hardy (itself based on a Victor Herbert opera in the early 1900's), and was also the name of a 1961 Disney musical starring Annette Funicello. However, when drummer Lori Barbero suggested the name, she thought it was the name of a children's book.

Barenaked Ladies

Founder members Ed Robinson and Steven Page had laughed together about this phrase, which refers to a child's innocent description of a nude woman, while watching a **Bob Dylan** concert, both agreeing it could be used for the name of a band.

Belle And Sebastian

Vocalist/Guitarist Stuart Murdoch had written a story about a girl named Belle and a boy named Sebastian, who got together and made records. The idea for the story was from a children's TV program, *Belle and Sebastian*, in the '60s about a young boy and his dog, made in France but shown (dubbed) on English TV. The TV show was itself based on a book by French author Mme. Cecile Aubry.

Black Crowes

Many references state that the group was originally named Mr. Crowe's Garden after a children's book of that name by Henry James, which name was suggested to them by a girl at a party. However, no such book by Henry James exists, and it is more likely that the reference is to *Johnny Crow's Garden*, written in 1903 by L. Leslie Brooke. The group added the "e" at the end of "crow" just to mess with people. The name change to Black Crowes came at the suggestion of Def American record label executive George Drakoulis, who prepared a list of alternatives, including The Confederate Crowes and The Stone Mountain Crowes, as well as Black Crowes.

BMX Bandits

BMX Bandits was the title of a 1983 teen movie starring Nicole Kidman, and although the members of the band were aware of the movie none of them had actually seen it. BMX (short for Bicycle Moto Cross) is the name of an ever-popular type of child's bicycle, and the name was chosen only half-seriously as it was felt the band would be short-lived.

Betty Boo

Born Alison Moira Clarkson, she originally used the stage name Betty Boop from her resemblance to the famous cartoon character. She later had to change her adopted stage name to Betty Boo after lawyers representing the interests of the cartoon character threatened legal action!

Circle Jerks

The term "circle jerk" refers to a group of young adolescents masturbating together in a circle, sometimes used during college frat house initiations.

Danny & The Juniors

Danny & The Juniors formed as a high school band called The Juvenaires, and featuring Danny Rapp on lead vocals. When signing with a record label, they were then renamed by Art Singer of Singular Records.

del Amitri

del Amitri's name is not in fact taken from the Greek translation of "from the womb" as is usually reported. Justin Currie (bass, vocals) has said that the name was simply three syllables (presumably he's referring to a–mi–tri) that he strung together while in the playground at school, although several other stories have been given to rock journalists over the years.

Thomas Dolby

Thomas Dolby was born Thomas Morgan Robertson, and was nicknamed "Dolby" by school friends because of his ever-present tape recorder, as most tape players incorporate the Dolby cassette noise reduction system. He was later sued by Dolby Laboratories and must now always use the full name, i.e. he can't use "Dolby" without the prefix "Thomas".

Adam Faith

Terence Nelhams-Wright thought for many years that his real name was Terence Nelhams, only to discover his birth name on applying for a passport (his father, Alf Nelhams, and mother, Ellen Wright, weren't married at the time of his birth registration). His stage name was taken from a book of boys' (Adam) and girls' (Faith) names owned by producer Jack Good, who suggested the name change and whose wife had just had a baby. Incidentally, Faith's mother and the mother of actor Michael Caine (*b.* Maurice Mickelwhite) actually worked together, but were unaware of the celebrity of their offspring, always referring to them by their real names!

Billy Idol

Born William Michael Albert Broad, his alter-ego was inspired by a written comment on one of his school reports. The teacher had written "WILLIAM IS IDLE", to which he thought "IDOL" as in "rock idol" would be more appropriate to him.

Kajagoogoo

The band wanted a nonsense name, so they adapted their name from "ga-ga-goo-goo", the sound attributed to babies. Limahl (vocals, bass) was born Chris Hamill, Limahl being an anagram of Hamill.

Frankie Lymon & The Teenagers

This group formed at high school under the original name of The Premiers, with Frankie Lymon on lead vocals. Their new name was suggested by bandleader Jimmy Wright during a recording session, in reference to the group members all being in their teens.

Lynyrd Skynyrd

The name Lynyrd Skynyrd was inspired by the band members' high school gym teacher, Mr Leonard Skinner, from whom they tried to cover up their long hair, only to be caught and repeatedly sent to the Principal. Band member Gary Rossington had quit school in protest, so fellow band member Ronnie Van Zant suggested changing the band name from One Percent as a tribute to that incident. Initially, the name was spelled Lynard Skynard, but then changed to its final form so as to avoid any possible trouble with the real Mr. Skinner.

Meat Loaf

Born Marvin Lee Aday, he was given the nickname "Meat" by his alcoholic father at a young age, adopting the stage name Meat Loaf as an extension of that. He sometimes told music journalists that a high school football coach had christened him "Meat Loaf" after he had stepped on his foot. He legally changed his real name to Michael Lee Aday (from Marvin) in 1983, saying that it was for personal reasons, and also that it suited his acting career better (he is billed as Michael Lee Aday in later films, rather than Meat Loaf). It has been rumored that the legal name change arose when Levi's put out a commercial with the punch line "Poor fat Marvin can't wear Levi's".

Moby Grape

Moby Grape was suggested by bass player Bob Mosley, and comes from the old children's joke which was doing the rounds in the '60s:- "What's purple and swims in the sea?"–"Moby Grape!".

New York Dolls

Existing references suggest that the band was named after the Russ Meyer soft-porn film, *Beyond the Valley of the Dolls*, as group members David Johansen and Arthur Kane had met at a screening of the movie. However, Kane had already decided on the band name prior to this meeting, taking it from the New York Dolls' Hospital, a trauma center for dolls. Johnny Thunders (guitar–*b.* John Anthony Genzale, Jr); Sylvain Sylvain (guitar, keyboards–*b.* Syl Mizrahl).

Poco

The band formed initially as Pogo, however they were forced to change to Poco following the threat of legal action by Walt Kelly, the creator of the Pogo Possum cartoon character.

Prefab Sprout

This name was thought up by group leader Paddy McAloon while at school, as he often saw older kids with albums by progressive rock groups with mysterious names like **Grateful Dead** and **Moby Grape**. He decided that in order to have a successful band he would need to come up with the most mysterious name he could think of, which ended up being Prefab Sprout. "Prefab" is an abbreviation for the pre-fabricated homes which were common after the Second World War in northern English towns such as Consett, Co. Durham, where McAloon was born. The group name was originally said to have been taken from a Nancy Sinatra song ("Jackson"), in which McAloon had apparently misheard the phrase "pepper sprout", although this explanation was later admitted to have been "pre-fabricated" by him.

Q-Tips

The Q-Tips were fronted by Paul Young, and their name was taken from the baby-care product of the same name. Young later formed a Tex-Mex band called Los Pacaminos, which is a play on the phrase "pack 'em in".

Rockwell

Born Kennedy Gordy (son of Motown label owner Berry Gordy), Rockwell had been the name of his high school band, which he later took as his solo stage name. He had changed his name to avoid charges of nepotism and was actually signed to Motown without his father's knowledge.

Shaggy

Shaggy was born Orville Richard Burrell, and was nick-named "Shaggy" by childhood friends in reference to the cartoon character in the children's TV series *Scooby Doo*, because of his slim build and tousled hair.

Sweet

Sweet were originally named Sweetshop, but later short-ened their name to Sweet. Brian Connolly (vocals) was born Brian Francis McManus, but on turning 18 discovered he had been adopted at birth, so from that point he took his birth mother's last name.

Thompson Twins

The Thompson Twins were named after the twin, bowler-hatted, bumbling, frightfully British detective characters in the children's animated TV series and comic books, *Herge's Adventures of Tin-Tin*. None of the band members are twins and none are named Thompson.

Was (Not Was)

The toddler son of Don Was (*b.* Don Fagenson) would say things like "Red, not red", when trying to describe opposites, so the band used that as inspiration for their stage name. They used the word "Was" as they expected their first record to also be their last, with main members Don and David Was changing their last names to reflect the band name. David Was (*b.* David Weiss).

Wings

The name Wings was inspired by the difficult birth of leader Paul McCartney's second child, Stella (now an internationally reknowned fashion designer). McCartney had imagined his unborn child being protected by angels and the word "wings" was uppermost in his mind. He later thought it would make a great name for a band.

Wonder Stuff

This name is often attributed to a comment made about vocalist Miles Hunt by John Lennon, a friend of Hunt's father, when he was a child ("The kid sure has the wonder stuff"). However, Hunt has since stated that this story was made up by a journalist friend of his, James Brown. Someone had called the house asking about the meaning of the band name, and Brown, pretending to be Hunt, made up the story related above.

I Dub Thee

Bands and artists whose names
were given to them

Apollonia

Apollonia was born Patricia Kotero, and was subsequently re-named by **Prince** when she started filming the movie *Purple Rain* (1984). Apollonia was the name of Michael Corleone's first wife in the movie *The Godfather* (1972), directed by Francis Ford Coppola.

Average White Band

Most references state that the name was jokingly given to them by Bonnie Bramlett (of Delaney & Bonnie fame), who used the band to back her on her first solo album, because of the unlikely combination of being Scottish and playing soul music. Actually, the name was inspired by a friend of lead vocalist and bass player Alan Gorrie's called Rob Wyper, who was a member of the British Diplomatic Service and often used the term "average white man" to compare conditions abroad, e.g. "too hot for the average white man", etc. Gorrie's girlfriend (later wife) suggested they use the name for the band.

B*Witched

Ray Hedges, their record company producer, kept telling them on first meeting them that they were very "bewitching", and it was Hedges that proposed using the name B*Witched. The '*' was added in place of the 'e' to make it look more like a logo.

B. Bumble & The Stingers

This name was chosen by record producer Kim Fowley for a session group who had recorded a rock version of Rimsky-Korsakov's "Flight Of The Bumble Bee", called "Bumble Boogie". After the song became a hit, an existing trio from Oklahoma was touted as being the "real" B Bumble & the

Stingers, with the story circulated in the music press that the leader was actually born William "Bill" Bumble.

Band

Previously known as The Hawks from early frontman Ronnie Hawkins, they were often referred to collectively as "the band" when they started backing **Bob Dylan**, and the name eventually stuck for their own recorded work. When they signed with Capitol they were first listed as The Crackers.

Beach Boys

The Beach Boys were originally called The Pendletons, after a type of shirt popular with youths at the time, then Kenny & the Cadets, with songwriter Brian Wilson representing Kenny. They were also at one time known as Carl and the Passions, after group member Carl Wilson, and this was later used as the title of a Beach Boys' album. Candix, their record company, changed their name to The Beach Boys without the group's consent in reference to their "surf music" recordings.

Brook Benton

Brook Benton was born Benjamin Franklin Peay, which is correctly pronounced "pee-ay", although so many people mispronounced it that he himself began pronouncing it as "pea". His stage name was suggested by Okeh record label A&R man Marv Halsman.

Bevis Frond

Bevis Frond is the alter-ego of Nick Saloman. He had initially wanted to name his band The Museum, but when walking home with school friend Julien Temple (who later achieved fame as a film director, including such movies as

Absolute Beginners (1986) and *Earth Girls Are Easy* (1989)), Temple suggested Bevis Frond instead. Saloman decided to combine the two names as Bevis Frond Museum, eventually using just Bevis Frond.

Big Audio Dynamite

Leader Mick Jones had already chosen the initials BAD for his new band when he left **The Clash**, but didn't have a name to go with it. While returning from a **Sigue Sigue Sputnik** gig, Yana, BAD's effects person, suggested using "Big Audio Dynamite" to fit the initials (Black And Decker has also been suggested as a good fit).

Blur

Blur were originally known as Seymour, from the character Seymour Glass who features in J. D. Salinger's novel *Franny And Zooey* (1961). However, their record label, Food Records, insisted that they change their name before they would sign them, and from a list of proposed alternatives the band chose Blur.

Box Tops

Initially known as The Devilles, they were forced to change on releasing their single "The Letter", as two previous groups had already released records as The Devilles. The name Box Tops was suggested by the group's manager, Roy Mack.

Chubby Checker

Born Ernest Evans, he was given the nickname "Chubby" by the proprietor of a produce store in which he worked as a teenager. The name Chubby Checker was suggested by *American Bandstand* presenter Dick Clark's wife Barbara, as a reference to **Fats Domino**.

Lou Christie

Lugee Alfredo Giovanni Sacco was re-christened Lou Christie by a Roulette Records company executive, a fact which Christie wasn't happy about–he had wanted to record under the single name Lugee.

Coolio

Born Artis Leon Ivey, Coolio acquired his nickname during a photo session where he was wearing a western-style shirt and playing a small guitar. This led someone to ask, "Who do you think you are, Coolio Iglesias?", a play on the name of the Spanish crooner, Julio Iglesias.

Christopher Cross

Christopher Cross was born Christopher Charles Geppert. He changed his name on releasing a single on a local Austin, Texas label, because Geppert was difficult to pronounce. He initially thought of using his middle name, i.e., Chris Charles, until someone at the session suggested using Chris Cross.

Dick Dale

Richard Anthony Monsour started out as a country music singer. His eventual stage name was put forward by a Texan disk jockey named T. Texas Tiny, who thought it would be a better name for a country star and also better for signing autographs.

Doris Day

Doris Day was born Doris Mary Ann von Kappelhoff, and was somewhat mercifully re-named for the stage by bandleader Barney Rapp, who was inspired when she sang "Day After Day" at an audition.

Dire Straits

Initially called The Café Racers after Dire Straits' founder member Mark Knopfler's previous band, they were re-named following a comment made by a friend of drummer Pick Withers about their rather desperate financial situation.

Lonnie Donnegan

Anthony Donnegan was inadvertently introduced early in his career as Lonnie Donnegan, when sharing the bill with blues guitarist Lonnie Johnson, and subsequently decided to keep the name.

En Vogue

En Vogue were brought together by the production team of Denzil Foster and Thomas McElroy, for a concept album they were making called *FM2*. The group was originally called For You, then they changed to Vogue, and finally to En Vogue on the discovery of an existing group called Vogue.

Georgie Fame

Georgie Fame was born Clive Powell, and was renamed by his manager, the well-known pop impresario Larry Parnes, on joining **Billy Fury**'s backing band The Blue Flames. The Blue Flames subsequently became Fame's own backing band.

Family

Originally called the Farinas and then briefly The Roaring Sixties, their new name Family was suggested by their record producer Kim Fowley, as a reference to their early Mafia-style gangster image.

Free

The name Free was suggested by Alexis Korner after his own '60s blues trio, Free At Last, when the band had just formed and was still without a name (Korner had just recommended teenage bass player Andy Fraser to them). Island Records label boss Chris Blackwell didn't like the name Free and had suggested Heavy Metal Kids, which the band in turn didn't like. Apparently the name Free caused problems at early gigs, as people would turn up expecting not to have to pay.

Billy Fury

Born Ronald Wycherley, Billy Fury's stage name was another creation of pop impresario Larry Parnes, who would typically re-name his stars with a normal first name and a strong last name (e.g. Fury, **Georgie Fame**, **Marty Wilde**, etc.).

Garbage

A friend of keyboards player Butch Vig's came into the studio to lay down some percussion on the remix of a **Nine Inch Nails** track (Vig at that time was a noted producer). Seeing all of the tape loops lying around apparently haphazardly, he commented that it looked like garbage and questioned whether Vig knew what he was doing. Vig decided to adopt the band name Garbage based on that brief exchange. Duke Erikson (guitars/bass/keyboards–b. Douglas Erikson); Butch Vig (keyboards–b. Bryan Vig).

Gene Loves Jezebel

Playing originally under the group name Slav Aryan, twins Michael and Jay Aston (b. John Peter Aston) had over time taken on the identities Gene and Jezebel. Mike had broken his leg playing soccer, and acquired the nickname Gene in reference to rock and roll singer Gene Vincent, who walked with a limp. The name Jezebel was adopted by Jay (who didn't identify with his birth name John) after being suggested by someone as an alternative. After a gig, an art student enquired of them "Did Gene love Jezebel?" and the name stuck for the group.

Genesis

Genesis were named by Jonathan King in recognition of it being the beginning of his production career. King's first proposal had been Gabriel's Angels, after Genesis vocalist Peter Gabriel. After the band took the name Genesis, it was discovered that a soul band of that name already existed in the US, so Revelations was considered as an alternative, until the US band broke up–the first album *Genesis and Revelations* (1969) was released without a band name on the album cover.

Peppermint Harris

Peppermint Harris was born Harrison D. Nelson Jr. and acquired the nickname "Peppermint" from the owner of a ballroom at which he had played. His first record showed his stage name as Peppermint Nelson, but when he came to record again the producer couldn't remember his name and, possibly confused over his actual first name of Harrison, he mis-remembered his stage name as Peppermint Harris.

Buddy Holly

Charles Hardin Holley was born the youngest of four children, and was known among the family as "Buddy", which was then a popular nickname for the youngest member of a family. His surname was misspelt as "Holly" on his first recording contract in 1956 with Decca Records, and he decided to keep it that way.

Hot Chocolate

Future Hot Chocolate vocalist Errol Brown sent a demo showcasing a reggae version of John Lennon's "Give Peace A Chance" to Apple Records, and the label decided to release it. Apple employee Mavis Smith suggested the name Hot Chocolate Band, which the group later shortened to Hot Chocolate.

Engelbert Humperdinck

Born Arnold George Dorsey, the first stage name he used was Gerry Dorsey, which was the name that he was popularly known by among friends and family. His final stage name was suggested by Tom Jones's manager, Gordon Mills, and was taken from the name of the 19th-century German classical composer best known for the opera *Hansel and Gretel*–Mills thought the new name would be more memorable; Las Vegas sign writers were eternally grateful.

Tab Hunter

Born Arthur Andrew Kelm, he was given his mother's maiden name Gelien at a young age when his parents divorced. He was re-named for the stage by his agent Harry Wilson who said, "We've got to tab you something", leading to the selection of the first name Tab. His last name came from his love of riding horses.

INXS

Originally formed as The Farriss Brothers, after members Andrew, Tim and Jon Farriss, their final name (which is pronounced as "in-excess"), was originally suggested as

"Inaccessible" by Gary Morris, manager of fellow-Australian band **Midnight Oil**.

Jefferson Airplane

The name Jefferson Airplane was taken from the name given by local blues musician Steve Talbot to his friend, Jefferson Airplane guitarist Jorma Kaukonen. Talbot called Kaukonen "Blind Thomas Jefferson Airplane", a tribute to bluesman Blind Lemon Jefferson. Marty Balin (*b*. Martyn Jerel Buchwald), changed his name in reference to the Bal Theater in San Leandro, California, on the advice of his manager.

Journey

Forming in San Francisco, Journey were originally named The Golden Gate Rhythm Section after the well-known local bridge and landmark. A local radio station ran a competition to re-name the band, but the final name was actually suggested by an associate of production manager Herbie Herbert.

Led Zeppelin

The name Led Zeppelin was inspired by a comment made by **Who**-drummer Keith Moon to describe nightmare gigs, i.e. "going down like a lead balloon". The group dropped the "a" from "lead" in order to prevent mis-pronunciation. John-Paul Jones (bass–*b*. John Baldwin) was re-named by **Rolling Stones** manager Andrew Loog-Oldham after a 1959 movie of that name starring Robert Stack and directed by John Farrow, about one of the founders of the US Navy. In 1970, the band played a gig in Copenhagen, Denmark as The Nobs, following a threat of legal action from Eva von Zeppelin over the unauthorized use of her family name.

Peggy Lee

Born Norma Deloris Egstrom of Swedish/Norwegian ancestry, her stage name was given to her by Ken Kennedy, the manager of Fargo, North Dakota radio station WDAY, because he thought she looked like a "Peggy".

Lulu

Born Marie McDonald McLaughlin Laurie, she was renamed Lulu by her manager Marion Massey, who had often referred to her as "a lulu of a kid", where "lulu" means a remarkable person.

Manic Street Preachers

The name was based on an incident that occurred while vocalist/guitarist James Dean Bradfield was busking, where a passing old man had remarked that he was a "manic street preacher". Nicky Wire (bass–b. Nicholas Allen Jones) acquired the nickname "The Wire" from his long (6' 4"), thin frame.

John Cougar Mellencamp

John Mellencamp was given the stage name Johnny Cougar by his manager, Tony DeFries, without his knowledge or consent, because DeFries did not think he would be successful under his own name. Mellencamp was unaware of it until his first album, *Chestnut Street Incident* (1976) was released with the name Johnny Cougar on the cover. *Johnny Cougar* was the name of a comic-strip "redskin" wrestler, which first appeared in the Tiger comic beginning in the 1970s. Mellencamp modified the original stage name to the not-so-young sounding John Cougar in 1979, then to John Cougar Mellencamp in 1983, and by 1991 was again using his own name of John Mellencamp.

Midnight Oil

The name Midnight Oil was suggested by original keyboard player Peter Watson (taken from the phrase "burning the midnight oil" referring to working into the small hours) and was chosen at random from other names that the band had suggested.

Guy Mitchell

Born Albert Cernick, he was renamed by Columbia Records' A&R man Mitch Miller (later to go onto recording fame in his own right), whose own given surname was really Mitchell. Miller thought he seemed like a "nice guy", so he was named Guy Mitchell.

Quiet Riot

Future Quiet Riot front man Kevin DuBrow used to hang out backstage after rock concerts, including UK rock legends **Status Quo** when they were trying to make it big in the States. One time when Quo guitarist Rick Parfitt and the band were drinking together after a gig, Parfitt was told by DuBrow that he intended to call his new band Little Women, to which Parfitt replied that if he was starting a new band he'd call them Quite Right. Because of Parfitt's London accent DuBrow mis-heard this as "Quiet Riot", and then decided to use that name for the new band he was forming.

Residents

The band had sent a demo to Warner Brothers, which was rejected. The record company did not have their names on file, only their address, so returned it marked "For the attention of the residents", so the group decided to use "The Residents" as their name.

Cliff Richard

Cliff Richard was born Harry Rodger Webb and his group's name was initially Harry Webb and the Drifters (later known as **The Shadows**). This was changed when Harry Greatorex, a promoter for the Regal Ballroom venue in Ripley (Derbyshire, UK) suggested to the group that they change the singer's name. Early Drifters band member Johnny Foster suggested Cliff Richards, after which fellow member Ian Samwell suggested leaving off the last "s" to make it more memorable.

Righteous Brothers

The Righteous Brothers were performing in a bar in Santa Ana, California as a 5-piece called The Paramours, when a US Marine in the audience yelled out at the end of the gig "That was righteous, brothers". The group's name was changed shortly after in recognition of the event.

Rose Royce

Formed initially as Total Concept Unlimited, they became Edwin Starr's backing band, then backed Yvonne Fair under the name Magic Wand. Eventually they met Motown composer Norman Whitfield, who re-named them Rose Royce, a pun on the famous British car maker, Rolls Royce. Rose Royce is actually the name of the group although it is often applied to lead singer Gwen Dickey, who is sometimes credited as Rose Norwalt (a name derived partly from the group name and partly from Norman Whitfield's name).

Sex Pistols

The Sex Pistols were originally called The Strands. "Sex" was at that time the name of manager Malcolm McLaren's shop in London's Kings Road (it is currently called "World's End", the old name for the poorer area around the southern end of the fashionable street), and "Sex Pistol" was a term coined by McLaren to describe a punk pin-up, or as he said, "a better-looking assassin". Johnny Rotten (vocals, *b.* John Lydon); Sid Vicious (bass, *b.* John Simon Ritchie).

Slade

Slade were originally formed as The N'Betweens, but changed their name at the request of Phillips Records to Ambrose Slade, a name which was proposed by their manager, Jack Baverstock, after he heard it in a TV movie he was watching. They later shortened the name to just Slade after a suggestion by their subsequent manager Chas Chandler. Noddy Holder (vocals, guitars–*b.* Neville Holder).

Sparks

Originally known as Halfnelson, which is a type of hold in wrestling, Sparks came from the initial suggestion of Sparks Brothers (like Marx Brothers) by record label boss Albert Grossman, but the band preferred just Sparks.

Spin Doctors

Initially formed as Trucking Company, the name Spin Doctors was suggested by guitarist Eric Schenkman. 'Spin doctor' is a term used for those election team members responsible for ensuring favorable publicity for their candidate–the band was formed during the 1988 US presidential election campaign. Chris Barron (vocals) *b.* Christopher Barron Gross).

Temptations

The Temptations changed from The Elgins when they signed to Motown subsidiary label, Miracle Records. The new name was quoted as being given to them by Motown boss Berry Gordy, although band member Otis Williams also claims credit for coming up with it while discussing alternatives with the other band members and Miracle employee Billy Mitchell. Another group had previously recorded under the name Temptations in the 1950s, but had since disbanded. Otis Williams (*b.* Otis Miles); Melvin Franklin was born David Melvin English, taking the name Franklin from his step-father Willard Franklin); David Ruffin (*b.* Davis Eli Ruffin).

Tribe Called Quest

A Tribe Called Quest's name was given to them by **Afrika Bambaata** of the band The Jungle Brothers, who attended the same New York high school as band members Q-Tip and DJ Ali Shaheed. Q-Tip (*b.* Jonathan Davis, now known as Kamaal Fareed after converting to Islam); Phife Dawg (*b.* Malik Taylor).

Tina Turner

Tina Turner was born Annie Mae Bullock, and later married R'n'B artist and record producer Ike Turner. Ike suggested she use the stage name Tina, inspired by Sheena Queen of the Jungle, the comic book heroine who first appeared in 1937.

Turtles

The Crossfires were re-named by their manager Reb Foster, initially as the Tyrtles (deliberately misspelt like **The**

Byrds), at the height of the British Invasion. The spelling was later changed to the regular Turtles. Howard Kaylan (vocals–*b*. Howard Kaplan) always wrote his original last name as Kaylan, so eventually he decided to formally change it.

Vanilla Fudge

Formed originally as The Pigeons, their new name was suggested by the female vocalist of a local band called The Unspoken Word, who loved vanilla fudge-flavored drumstick ice cream cones.

Vanity 6

Vanity 6 were named for lead vocalist Vanity (*b*. Denise Matthews), so named by Prince because she reminded him of looking in a mirror and seeing a kindred soul. Prince apparently at first wanted to call the group The Hookers or, more controversially, Vagina Sex, but settled on Vanity 6.

Marty Wilde

Marty Wilde was born Reginald Smith, and although he had already changed his last name to Patterson, he was re-named by manager Larry Parnes following his aforementioned strong last name formula.

Members Only

Bands whose names were inspired by
one or more of their members

ABBA

Abba's name is formed from the initial letters of the four group members Christian names (Agnetha, Benny, Bjorn and Annafried). After early gigs as Festfolket (Swedish for "Engaged Couples"), they recorded as Bjorn, Benny, Agnetha & Frida. ABBA was then suggested by the group's mentor and label boss, Stig Anderson. They later discovered that Abba was also the name of Sweden's largest fish-canning company, who happily gave permission for the band to carry on using the name. Rather than objecting and threatening legal action, the canning company sent the group a gift of a case of tuna. This discovery is also the reason one of the "B"'s in the group's name is reversed in the logo.

Adverts

Bass player Gaye Advert was born Gaye Atlas, and was inadvertently re-named by The Stranglers, who were adding her name to their guest list but couldn't remember her last name. The band then took their handle from her new last name. TV Smith (b. Tim Smith).

Alan Parsons Project

Originally inspired by Al Stewart, the Project is actually a partnership between musician Alan Parsons and song-writer Eric Woolfson. The name is an ironic comment on the fact that their first album took two years to make.

Allman Brothers

The Allman Brothers are named after the founder members, brothers Greg and Duane (b. Howard Duane) Allman. Initially the band was known as the Allman Joys (like the chocolate bar Almond Joy), then Almanac, before renaming to Hour Glass and finally settling on Allman Brothers.

Band Of Susans

Initially three members of the band were called Susan (Susan Lyall, Susan Stenger and Susan Tallman), so the name Band of Susans began as an inside joke and stuck.

Beastie Boys

MCA (Master of Ceremonies Adam–*b*. Adam Yauch) had worn a badge with "Beastie Boys" written on it, following a name game with guitarist John Berry. "B-Boys" is used collectively for those who are into Hip-Hop. Several sources suggest that the name is an acronym for "Boys Entering Anarchistic States Toward Internal Excellence", however it is likely that this was invented later to fit the existing letters. Mike D (*b*. Michael Diamond); Ad-Rock (*b*. Adam Horowitz).

Belly

When singer/guitarist Tanya Donnelly left the bands she was simultaneously involved with (Throwing Muses and **The Breeders**), she named her new group Belly, apparently her favorite word.

Ben Folds Five

Led by Ben Folds, The Ben Folds Five are actually a trio. Folds has said that Ben Folds Five sounds better than Ben Folds Three, which cannot be argued with.

Big Head Todd & The Monsters

This group was named at high school (the now infamous Columbine in Colorado) and is named partially for guitarist and founder member Todd Park Mohr, and partially for blues legend Eddie "Clean Head" Vinson. "Monsters" was added as a sardonic comment on ostentatious band names.

Blondie

Originally called Angel and the Snake, Debbie Harry suggested the change of name to Blondie based on the many sexist comments which were directed at her, when she was invariably referred to as "Blondie".

Bon Jovi

Bon Jovi are named after lead vocalist Jon Bon Jovi (*b.* John Francis Bongiovi, Jr.). Keyboards player David Bryan was born David Bryan Rashbaum.

Brian Auger Trinity

Originally a threesome known as The Brian Auger Trio after leader Brian Auger, they became known as the Brian Auger Trinity after guitarist John McLaughlin and sax player Glen Hughes joined, expanding their number to five. Auger has said in an interview that "trinity" referred to a combination of three musical styles: blues, Motown and [Jazz] Messengers.

C & C Music Factory

C & C Music Factory were named in reference to the last name initials of founder members/producers Robert Clivillés and David Cole.

Damned

The Damned were named by guitarist Brian James from a 1969 movie of that name about pre-Nazi Germany, starring Dirk Bogarde and directed by Luchino Visconti. After the original group split, several members reformed as The

Doomed for a while, before reverting back to the original name. Dave Vanian (vocals–*b*. David Letts) changed his name because he thought Letts was too abrupt–he was also known as Dave Zero for a short period; Captain Sensible (bass–*b*. Raymond Ian Burns), was christened by Larry Wallis of the Pink Fairies for pouring beer over himself during a French punk rock festival; drummer Rat Scabies (*b*. Chris Miller) acquired his own stage name while he actually had scabies, a skin disease–at the time he was auditioning for punk rock group London SS, when a rat ran in front of him, and Mick Jones (later of the **Clash**) shouted "Rat, Scabies!"; Brian James (guitars–*b*. Brian James Robertson).

Danzig

Danzig are named for frontman Glenn Danzig, who was born Glenn Allen Anzalone–Danzig was formerly the name of a port city in Germany, now called Gdansk and part of Poland since World War II. Danzig's previous band, *The Misfits*, was named for the 1961 movie which was Marilyn Monroe's (and Clark Gable's) final film, directed by John Huston.

Dave Dee, Dozy, Beaky, Mick & Tich

Originally known as Dave Dee & the Bostons, they changed their name based on the group member's nicknames: David Harman (Dave Dee), Trevor Davies (Dozy), John Dymond (Beaky), Michael Wilson (Mick) and Ian Amey (Tich).

Dio

Dio were named after lead vocalist Ronnie James Dio (*b*. Ronald James Padavona), who chose his stage name after Johnny Dio (*b*. John DioGuardi), a member of the crime syndicate enforcement squad which was known as Murder Inc.

D-Mob

D-Mob are named for mixer Dancin' Danny D (b. Daniel Kojo Poku), the main creative force behind the name, who also released records as The Taurus Boys.

dodgy

The band dodgy started out as the feature act of "The dodgy Club", a mix of bands and DJs brought together in one club in Kingston-upon-Thames, London, before they branched out to gigs at other venues.

Dr Hook & The Medicine Show

This name was invented on the fly by guitarist George Cummings when a Bandbox, New Jersey club owner demanded a name for a poster advertising a gig. "Dr Hook" came from drummer Ray Sawyer, wearing a Captain Hook-like eye-patch, "medicine show" being a reference to the high profile of drugs at that time.

Eddie & The Hot Rods

'Eddie' was the name of a dummy that the band used to abuse during their stage act. It started out one Guy Fawkes Night as a joke, after the band had seen kids going door-to-door with their "guys". They made a 6' 6" guy and propped him up on stage, referring to him as Eddie as if he was a member of the band. Guy Fawkes Night is a UK festival every 5th November, celebrating the plot by Guy Fawkes in 1605 to blow up the Houses of Parliament. Kids make "guys" from old clothes stuffed with rags and go door-to-door for money and sweets.

England Dan & John Ford Coley

Dan Seals acquired the nickname "England" when, as a child, he was obsessed with the Beatles and would fake a British accent. John Ford Coley was born John Colley, but dropped one "l" from his last name to aid pronunciation. The duo were originally known as Colley & Wayland (Wayland is Seals' middle name).

EPMD

The name EPMD is formed from the duo's nicknames: Erick Sermon is known as E Double E, and Parrish Smith is known as Pee MD. One source states that the initials stand for Eric and Parrish Making Dollars!

Fat Boys

The Fat Boys, with a combined weight of over 750 lbs (more than 53 stones), were originally known as the Disco 3, but changed their name when their manager, Charles Stettler, complained about excessive food bills while they were touring. Prince Markie Dee (*b.* Mark Morales); Kool Rock Ski (*b.* Damon Wimbley); Buff Love The Human Beat Box (*b.* Darren Robinson),

Fat Larry's Band

Fat Larry's Band were named after their drummer, 'Fat' Larry James, and were also known as The Magic of the Blue, a variation on their previous name of Blue Magic.

Foreigner

The name Foreigner was inspired by the dual nationality (three British members and three American) of the band at its inception, and was suggested by original member

Mick Jones to the band's manager, Bud Prager. Lou Gramm (vocals–b. Lou Grammatico)

Gerry & The Pacemakers

The group was originally called the Mars Bars, from the first part of lead vocalist Gerry and brother Fred Marsden's last name, in an effort to gain corporate sponsorship, but was forced to change by the Mars confectionery group. Gerry Marsden got the idea for the name Pacemakers after watching a track event on TV, when the commentator referred to one of the runners as a "pacemaker", one who sets the pace for the others to follow.

Grant Lee Buffalo

Using various names at first, including The Machine Elves and Rex Mundi, they eventually settled on Grant Lee Buffalo, named for singer/guitarist Grant Lee Phillips and also representing American historical characters, such as Buffalo Bill.

Guru Josh

Guru Josh was born Paul Walden, and his stage name derives from his goatee beard (making him look like a "guru") with part of the name of his previous band, Joshua Cries Wolf.

Hawkwind

Originally billed as Group X when they hadn't yet thought of a permanent name, Hawkwind's final name (which appeared first on record as Hawkwind Zoo) was inspired partly as a joke at the expense of original band member Nik Turner, who had a hawk-like nose and (supposedly) regularly broke wind, and partly by Hawkmoon, a character developed by UK science-fiction writer Michael Moorcock.

Heavy D & The Boyz

Heavy D is the stage name of Dwight Myers, who describes himself as the "overweight lover of rap from money earnin' Mount Vernon". He kept the prefix "Heavy" even after he had lost 135 lbs (almost 10 stones) in weight in order to further his acting career.

Honeycombs

Originally the Sherabons, they were re-named The Honeycombs after signing to Pye Records and starting to work with British producer, Joe Meek. The new name was taken from female drummer Ann Lantree (very rare at that time), who was nicknamed "Honey", with 'combs' being added in reference to the previous occupation of another band member as a hairdresser. Vocalist Dennis D'Ell (b. Dennis Dalziel).

J Geils Band

Initially called the J Geils Blues Band after guitarist Jerome Geils, they later dropped "blues" from the band name. Vocalist Peter Wolf (b. Peter Blankfield) was nicknamed "Little Wolf" by his grandmother; Magic Dick (harmonica– b. Richard Salwitz).

Jam & Spoon

Jam & Spoon are named after producer Jam El Mar (b. Rolf Ellmer) and DJ Mark Spoon (b. Markus Löffel–"löffel" is German for "spoon"). They have also recorded under the names Tokyo Ghetto Pussy and Storm, using the pseudonyms Trancy Spacer and Spacey Trancer.

James

James formed originally as Venereal & The Diseases, and then changed to Volume Distortion, followed by one gig as Model Team International. For the first gig in which they used a variation of the name James they were billed as "James (Not A Poet)". The name James was suggested by original guitarist Paul Gilbertson, inspired by his admiration for Orange Juice guitarist James Kirk.

Little Feat

Leader Lowell George was previously with **Frank Zappa's Mothers of Invention**, and the name Little Feat came from comments made by Mothers' drummer Jimmy Carl Black about the size of George's feet. The band changed the spelling of "feet" to "feat" as a play on words.

M/A/R/R/S

M/A/R/R/S/ was a collaboration of dance groups Colourbox and A R Kane that came together for one single only ("Pump Up The Volume"). Like **Abba**, the name is a mnemonic taken from the first names of those involved with the project: Martyn Young–Colourbox, Alex Ayuli–A R Kane, Rudi Tambala–A R Kane, Russell (an A R Kane associate) and Steve Young–Colourbox.

Manfred Mann

The band Manfred Mann was originally known as the Mann-Hugg Blues Band, after founder members Manfred Mann and Mike Hugg. HMV Records producer John Burgess suggested that the band change their name to just Manfred Mann, which was not popular with Mann himself. Mann (reported variously as being born Michael/Manfred Liebowitz/Lubowitz) had initially used the pseudonym Manfred Manne (taking Manne from band-leader and drummer Shelly Manne) when writing for Jazz News magazine. After Manfred Mann (the band) broke up, Manfred Mann (the man) started a new project tentatively called Emanon ("no name" spelled backwards), which became Chapter III, then finally Manfred Mann's Earthband. Paul Jones (vocals–b. Paul Pond).

Martha & The Muffins

Formed in 1977, the band specifically wanted a name which would not be suggestive of the violent punk names of the time, and The Muffins was suggested as fitting the bill. Lead vocalist and organist Martha Johnson's name was then prefixed to the name.

Mink DeVille

Originally formed as Billy DeSade and the Marquis, Mink DeVille was re-named after leader Willy DeVille (vocals, guitars–b. William Borsay or Borsey).

Peaches & Herb

"Peaches" was the nickname of the original female half of the duo, Francine Hurd, which she acquired as a caring and sensitive child. Herb was Herb Fame (b. Herbert Feemster). The original Peaches has been replaced by different female vocalists through time, although they always recorded under the name Peaches; Herb has remained unchanged.

Phish

Phish first appeared under the name The Blackwood Convention, before changing their name to Phish, which was inspired by drummer John Fishman (nicknamed "Fish"). Ben & Jerry's ice-cream flavor "Phish Food" was named as a tribute to the band. Trey Anastacio (guitars–b. Ernest Guiseppe Anastacio III).

Police

The name Police was suggested by Stewart Copeland and was inspired by his father's former profession, being a member of the United States Central Intelligence Agency (CIA). Andy Summers (guitars–b. Andrew James Somers) changed his name because the phonetic "summers" was easier for people to spell. See also **Sting**.

Ronettes

The Ronettes formed originally as Ronnie & The Relatives, featuring Veronica Bennett ("Ronnie" being the familiar form of Veronica), sister Estelle and cousin Nedra Talley. They later changed their name to The Ronettes at the suggestion of their mother Beatrice, in order to more closely resemble the hit groups of the time, e.g. The Marvelettes.

Run DMC

Run DMC takes its name from rappers Joseph "Run" Simmons and MC Darryl "D" McDaniels (D-MC). Run acquired his nickname, originally as "Kurtis Blow's Disco Son DJ Run", when spinning records for Kurtis Blow (who was managed by Simmons's older brother, Russell). The nickname was later shortened to "Run Love" then simply "Run". D-MC was originally known as "Easy D". DJ Jam Master Jay (b. Jason Mizell) was earlier known as "Jazzy Jase".

Sly & Robbie

Sly & Robbie are respectively Sly Dunbar (b. Lowell Charles Dunbar) and Robert "Robbie" Shakespeare. Sly acquired his nickname from his appreciation of funk musician, **Sly Stone**.

Smokie

After several early names, the band re-named themselves Smokey in reference to vocalist Chris Norman's voice, but later changed the spelling to avoid legal action from Motown recording star Smokey Robinson.

Soul II Soul

Soul II Soul was originally the name of Jazzie B's mobile sound system, which he formed with friends Daddae Harvey and Aitch B to play at parties and youth clubs in London. The name eventually became a brand, applying to both fashion and music, and was later also adopted as the name of Jazzie B's band. Jazzie B (*b.* Beresford Romeo) acquired his nickname at school from his habit of interspersing his reggae dubs with jazz-funk tracks.

Springfields

The Springfields chose their name from original member Tim Field's surname, extending "Field" to "Springfield" so that it sounded more American. Dusty Springfield (*b.* Mary Isobel Catherine Bernadette O'Brien), and her brother Tom (*b.* Dion O'Brien), adopted the group's name as their last name. Dusty acquired her nickname as a child because of her tomboyish behavior. Mike Hurst (*b.* Michael Longhurst-Pickworth).

Tenpole Tudor

Tenpole Tudor took their name from vocalist Eddie Tenpole (*b.* Edward Tudor-Pole), who later moved into TV as the presenter of UK ITV Channel 4's game show, *The Crystal Maze*.

TLC

TLC take their name from the initial letters of the three group members nicknames. T-Boz (b. Tionne Tenise Watkins) was known as "The Boss" when the group first formed, which was later shortened to T-Boz. Left Eye (b. Lisa Nicole Lopes) was so-called because she occasionally wore a condom over her left eye to advocate safe sex. Chilli (b. Rozonda Ocelean Thomas), who had replaced Crystal, the original "C" of TLC, was given her nickname by T-Boz and Left Eye.

Toots & The Maytals

Toots & The Maytals are named after lead vocalist Frederick Nathaniel "Toots" Hibbert, nicknamed as a baby. The group name Maytals was inspired by his hometown, May Pen, in the parish of Clarendon, Jamaica.

Wah!

Wah! was taken from something the group's founder member Pete Wylie said ("Wah! Heat!"), when cycling to Eric's Club in his home city of Liverpool, wearing a leather jacket on a hot day. The band has since used other variations of the Wah! name, including "Wah! Heat", "Shambeko Say Wah!", "Pete Wylie and Wah! The Mongrel", and "The Mighty Wah!".

Nom de Plume

Artists whose stage names are
variations of their given name

2PAC

2PAC was born Lesane Parish Crooks, following which his mother, political activist Alice Faye Walker, re-married and took her new husband's (Lumumba Shakur) Moslem surname, becoming Afeni Shakur. She renamed her son Tupac Amaru Shakur (which means "shining serpent, blessed one") in 1972, then moved in with Lumumba's brother Mutulu after Lumumba left her. Tupac also recorded as Makaveli, having read and been inspired by 16th-century Italian politician and philosopher Niccolo Machiavelli, while in prison.

Beck

Beck Hansen was born Beck David Campbell, the son of noted concertmaster and arranger David Campbell. When his parents split, he took the surname of his mother, the actress and former Andy Warhol protégé Bibbe Hansen.

Björk

Björk was born Björk Gudmundsdôttir in Iceland. She once played with a band called Tappi Tikarrass, which translates as "cork [or plug] the bitch's ass", a name derived from a comment made about their music by the bass player's father.

Blind Blake

Born Arthur Blake, he was blind from birth. Some reference sources have reported that his given name was Phelps–however, he is quoted in a recorded interview with

Papa Charlie Jackson as saying that his given name is Blake.

Belinda Carlisle

Although Belinda Carlisle is her real name (having been named after a character from her mother's favorite movie, *Johnny Belinda* (1948)) she had her name changed to that of her stepfather (Kurczeski) at age 7. As she subsequently reverted to her birth name at 17, some references incorrectly state that she was born Belinda Kurczeski.

Johnny Cash

Johnny Cash was born J. R. Cash (initials only, no first or second names). He eventually acquired the name John, although the "R" remained an initial and doesn't actually stand for anything. Cash was annoyed that Sam Philips of Sun Records had billed him on his first record as "Johnny", as he thought it made him sound too young (he was by that time 23).

Ray Charles

Ray Charles was born Ray Charles Robinson. Initially he used his given name Ray Robinson for the stage. He later shortened his stage name to Ray Charles in order to avoid confusion with boxer, "Sugar" Ray Robinson.

Eagle-Eye Cherry

Eagle-Eye is the son of jazz trumpeter Don Cherry and brother of **Neneh Cherry**. Eagle-Eye is actually his real name, and was given to him by his father on first seeing his newborn son, because he was looking at him with only one eye open.

Neneh Cherry

Neneh Cherry was born Neneh Mariann Karlsson. Her parents were Swedish artist Moki Karlsson and Ahmadu Jah, an African musician, however she was raised by her mother Moki and step-father Don Cherry, the renowned jazz trumpeter. Moki had met Cherry shortly after Neneh's birth, and Neneh took her step-father's name.

Eric Clapton

Born Eric Patrick Clapton, the son of Patricia Clapton (who was 16 at the time) and Edward Fryer, he was raised by his grandmother, Rose, and her second husband, Jack Clapp, as their own son (interestingly he referred to them as Mum and Dad, and thought his mother was his sister). As a result he is often reported as having been born Eric Patrick Clapp.

Terence Trent D'Arby

Born Terence Trent Darby (with no apostrophe), he recently changed his name to Sananda Maitreya. "Sananda" came from a series of dreams where angels called to him using that name, while Maitreya comes from the myth of a world teacher (the fifth Buddha) who will one day return to this world to re-establish the teachings of the Buddha. He has also recorded as The Incredible E.G. O'Reilly.

Des'ree

Born as Desiree Weekes, she wanted a first name with only two syllables and so dropped the "i" to become simply Des'ree.

Neil Diamond

Born Neil Leslie Diamond, his real name is sometimes given as Noah Kaminsky, which at one time he considered using as a stage name, because he didn't like his own name–another name he considered for the stage was Ice Cherry.

Bob Dylan

Bob Dylan was born Robert Allan Zimmerman. He has claimed various sources for his stage name over the years, including being inspired by Welsh poet Dylan Thomas, however the most likely version has him naming himself in honor of his uncle, Dillion.

Enya

Enya was born Eithne Ni Bhraonain, Enya being the English spelling of her christian name.

Noosha Fox

Noosha Fox had previously recorded with the group Wooden Horse using her real name of Susan Traynor. She adopted the stage name Noosha (a variation of the letters of her real first name re-arranged, i.e. "nussa") when she joined the band Fox.

Connie Francis

Connie Francis was born Concetta Rosa Maria Franconero, which she changed after a suggestion by TV talent show host Arthur Godfrey.

Marvin Gaye

Marvin Gaye was born Marvin Pentz Gay–he was sensitive about his last name and so added the "e".

Jimi Hendrix

At birth, Hendrix's mother Lucille gave him the name Johnny Allen Hendrix, however his father Al Hendrix (who was away serving with the U.S. military during the Second World War) was unaware of this. Later his father returned from active duty and legally changed his son's name to James Marshall Hendrix when he was 3 years old. Hendrix had previously performed under the stage name Jimmy James, but changed the spelling of his first name to "Jimi" at the suggestion of his manager Chas Chandler on forming the Jimi Hendrix Experience, to make it more memorable.

Joan Jett & The Blackhearts

Sources invariably state that Joan Jett was born Joan Marie Larkin, however in interviews she has refuted this, confirming that Joan Jett is her real name. The group name, Blackhearts, was inspired by the idea of a graffiti logo that could be drawn on a bathroom wall, featuring a heart completely blocked out in black.

Patti Labelle

Patti Labelle was born Patricia Louise Holt. She adopted her stage name on forming the Blue Belles, who were named by producer Bobby Martin after a local record label, Bluebell Records.

k d lang

Born Kathryn Dawn Lang, she uses the lower case form of her name because, as she herself has said in the past, "Its generic and, unlike Cherry Bomb, its a name, not a sexuality".

Gary Lewis

Gary Lewis was the leader of Gary Lewis & the Playboys, and was born Gary Harold Lee Levitch–he is the son of comedian Jerry Lewis (*b.* Jerome Levitch). His name was changed to Lewis when he was only two years old.

Tony Orlando & Dawn

Michael Anthony Orlando Cassivitis (*AKA* Tony Orlando) was working as a General Professional Manager with April-Blackwood Music when he was offered a demo of the song "Candida". He tried to place it with Bell Records, however Bell rejected it because of the original vocal. Orlando agreed to re-record it with himself singing the lead, but April-Blackwood would not allow him to use his name on the record, so he chose the pseudonym Dawn, after the name of his production manager's daughter.

Gram Parsons

Born Ingram Cecil Connor III, Gram is short for Ingram. His mother was later re-married to Robert Parsons, who adopted Gram thus changing his last name to Parsons.

Michelle Shocked

Born Michelle Karen Johnston, in her early twenties she was sent to a psychiatric hospital and diagnosed with paranoid schizophrenia. Part of her treatment involved electric shock therapy, and she adopted the name Michelle Shocked after her release from the hospital.

Donna Summer

Donna Summer was born LaDonna Andrea Gaines, but changed her name when she married Austrian actor

Helmut Sommer, retaining the Anglicized version of his last name after a misprint on her first single on the Georgio Moroder-owned Oasis label, "The Hostage".

Also Known As

Bands and artists whose names
are based on nicknames

Babyface

Born Kenneth Edmonds, he was playing guitar one day with a band called The Deele at the QCA recording studio in Cincinnati, when **Bootsy Collins**, ex-bass guitarist with James Brown's Famous Flames and Parliment/Funkadelic, walked in. Collins yelled out to him, "There's Babyface!", referring to his youthful looks, and everyone in the band picked up on it.

Ginger Baker

Ginger Baker was born Peter Edward Baker, and was nicknamed at an early age for his hair colour, later deciding to keep the nickname as his stage name.

Long John Baldry

Long John Baldry was born John Baldry, with the nickname "Long John" coming from his exceptional 6'7" (2.01m) height.

Barbecue Bob

Born Robert Hicks, he had spent some time working at Tidwell's Barbecue in the Atlanta suburb of Buckhead where he was discovered by Columbia Records scout, Dan Hornsby. After he moved to New Orleans, Hornsby gave him the stage name Barbecue Bob in reference to his earlier job.

Syd Barrett

Roger Keith Barrett (founding member of **Pink Floyd**) was nicknamed "Syd" in honor of a bass player who played at his teenage hangout, the Anchor Coffee Bar (home of the Riverside Jazz Club) in the Mill Pond area of his hometown of Cambridge, England.

Count Basie

Count Basie was born William Basie and adopted the stage name "Count" when he took over Bennie Moten's band (known as the Barons of Rhythm) in Kansas City in the mid-1930s. The name was a promotional gimmick to rival the "Duke" (**Duke Ellington**) and the "Earl" (Earl "Fatha" Hines).

Big Bopper

The Big Bopper was born Jiles Perry Richardson, and was known to his friends as "J.P." or "Jape" for short. He took his stage name while presenting a music show on radio station KTRM in Beaumont, Texas after he saw all the kids doing a dance called "The Bop".

Bluebells

Leader Robert Hodgens was nicknamed "Bobby Bluebell", "Bluebell" being a Scottish brand of matches. In 1984, the band fought with another band, The Bluebells Of Paris, for the rights to use the name.

Bo Diddley

Bo Diddley was born Otha Ellas Bates, but was later adopted by his mother's cousin Gussie McDaniel, and renamed Ellas McDaniel (sometimes quoted as Elias). His nickname "Bo Diddley" came from a comment made by a girl who witnessed a childhood fight (a "bo-diddley" was street slang for a bully), and he kept the name when he started boxing and also for his stage career.

Boy George

Boy George's real name is George Alan O'Dowd. He began using the stage name Boy George on forming the band In

Praise Of Lemmings in 1981. He also appeared in the band **Bow Wow Wow** under the stage name Lieutenant Lush.

Buckwheat Zydeco

Born Stanley Joseph Dural Jr., he was nicknamed "Buckwheat" by his friend Eddie Taylor due to his likeness to the character of that name in the TV show *The Little Rascals*. Zydeco is a form of Southern US music originally sung in Creole, and is thought to be a variation on the French word for beans, "les haricots". Buckwheat began to play the zydeco accordion and changed his stage name in honor of that instrument.

Captain & Tennille

When touring with **The Beach Boys** as part of their backing band, Daryl Dragon acquired the nickname "Captain Keyboard" from Beach Boys vocalist Mike Love, because of his habit of wearing a naval officers cap on stage. He later formed a duo with another member of the backing band, vocalist Toni Tennille.

Chaka Demus & Pliers

Chaka Demus, who was born John Taylor, originally took the stage name Nicodemus Jr. in honor of the great 1980s Jamaican MC, Nicodemus, but later changed to Chaka Demus to be more original. Pliers (*b.* Everton Bonner) acquired the nickname Pliers because of his similarity to another Jamaican performer of the time, Pinchers. Pliers has two brothers, Joseph Anthony Bonner, who performs as Spanner Banner in reference to his brother's stage name, and Richell Bonner, who performs as Richie Spice.

China Crisis

The name China Crisis was inspired by member Eddie Lundon's childhood nickname of "Chink", referring to his slightly oriental looks ("Chink" is a disparaging nickname which is sometimes applied to Chinese people in the UK).

Bootsy Collins

Bootsy Collins, ex-bass player with James Brown's Famous Flames and George Clinton's Parliament-Funkadelic, was born William Collins. His mother bestowed his nickname upon him because, as she said, he looked like a Bootsy.

Chick Corea

Chick Corea was born Armando Anthony Corea. His nickname came from his aunt's habit of pinching his cheek as a child, and the name stuck.

Skeeter Davis

Skeeter Davis was born Mary Frances Penick. She was nicknamed "Skeeter", after the local Kentucky term for a mosquito, by her grandfather because she was always buzzing around like an insect. She later adopted the last name Davis when she formed the Davis Sisters with school friend Betty Jack Davis, keeping the name when she went solo.

Fats Domino

Born Antoine Domino, he was nicknamed Fats following the release of his first single in 1950, a song called "The Fat Man".

Dr Dre

Dr Dre was born Andre Young, "Dre" being short for Andre. He was a fan of basketball star Julius Erving, known as Dr J, and adopted the prefix "Dr" for his own stage name.

Champion Jack Dupree

Champion Jack Dupree was born William Thomas Dupree in New Orleans. After moving to Detroit he was introduced to heavyweight boxing champion Joe Louis, who helped him start out as a boxer. He went on to become lightweight champion of Indiana, which earned him the nickname of "Champion Jack", probably in tribute to a former boxing champion, heavyweight Jack Johnson.

Duke Ellington

Born Edward Kennedy Ellington, he was nicknamed "Duke" by a childhood friend because of his regal manner, and decided to keep it as his stage name.

Fresh Prince

Born Willard Christopher "Will" Smith II, he acquired the nickname "Prince" as a child, because he could always charm his way out of trouble. This was expanded to "Fresh Prince" for his stage name, and was used in the NBC TV comedy show *The Fresh Prince Of Bel Air*, which aired between 1990 and 1996.

Dizzy Gillespie

Dizzy Gillespie was born John Birks Gillespie, and was nicknamed Dizzy by trumpeter Fats Palmer in reference to his exuberant personality. Gillespie had saved Palmer's life when he was overcome by gas fumes while they were on tour together.

Goldie

Goldie was born Clifford Price, and earned the nickname "Goldilocks", which later became shortened to Goldie, when he grew Rastafarian dreadlocks. The nickname, which he adopted as his stage name, did not come from selling engraved gold teeth in Miami, as is often reported, because by that time he had already acquired the name. He also recorded as Rufige Kru and MetalHeadz, the latter also being the name of his record label.

Grandmaster Flash & the Furious Five

Grandmaster Flash was born Joseph Saddler, acquiring the nickname Flash from his lightning-fast mixing techniques, and adopting the prefix Grand Master in homage to kung fu movie star Bruce Lee. The Furious Five were five rap artists who rapped over Grandmaster Flash's mixing–Melle Mel was born Melvin Glover; Cowboy (b. Keith Wiggins) acquired his nickname from his bow legs, looking like he just got off a horse; Kid Creole (b. Nathaniel Glover, brother of Melle Mel); Rahiem (b. Guy Todd Williams); Scorpio (b. Eddie Morris, AKA Mr Ness).

Iggy Pop

Iggy Pop was born James Newell Osterburg, and adopted the nickname Iggy while playing drums for The Iguanas, a local band in Ann Arbor, Michigan. When he first joined The Stooges (known at that time as The Psychedelic Stooges) he became known as Iggy Stooge, adopting the suffix "Pop" later, after a friend named Jim Popp, more than a reference to pop music.

Jodeci

The name Jodeci is taken from the band members' nicknames–Jo Jo (*b.* Joel Hailey), DeVante Swing (*b.* Donald Earle DeGrate Jr), K-Ci (*b.* Cedric Hailey), Mr Dalvin (*b.* Dalvin DeGrate Jr).

Kid Rock

Born Robert James Ritchie near Detroit, his nickname was acquired when he used to spin and scratch records at house parties, where people would exclaim things like, "Look at that kid rock!").

B.B. King

Born Riley B. King, he had a job working as a DJ for a Memphis radio station WDIA. As his show King's Spot became more popular, it was decided that he needed a more interesting name. His first radio name was "The Beale Street Blues Boy" (after Beale Street in Memphis, a famous gathering spot for performing blues artists), which was shortened first to "Blues Boy" then simply "B.B.". The middle initial "B" in his real name, Riley B. King, is just an abbreviation; it doesn't actually stand for anything. Interestingly, his first name was originally intended to be "O'Riley", after a local Irish plantation owner named Jim O'Reilly, but his father decided to leave off the "O".

Kool & The Gang

"Kool" is the nickname of bass player Robert Bell, who is now known by his Moslem name of Amir Bayan (his brother Ronald Bell, also in the group, is now known as Khalis Bayan). The band went through several name changes, having originally formed as The Jazziacs followed by the New Dimensions, then the Soul Town Band, followed by Kool & the Flames, after their promoter designed a poster with that name on it. They finally changed to Kool & The Gang to avoid confusion with James Brown's band, The Famous Flames.

Leadbelly

Born Huddie William Ledbetter, he acquired the nickname "Leadbelly" because of his toughness, while serving time in Louisiana State Penitentiary.

Little Richard

Little Richard was born Richard Wayne Penniman, and was afflicted with a short arm and a short leg. Sources have claimed his physical affliction as the origin of his nickname, but in interviews he has said that it was simply a childhood name given to him as one of the smallest of 14 children.

Muddy Waters

Born McKinley Morganfield, he was nicknamed Muddy by his grandmother after his habit of playing in the marshes and waters around his home in the Mississippi delta. He added the suffix "Water" when he became a performer, expanding that to "Waters" when he migrated north to Chicago.

Cozy Powell

Born Colin Powell, he was given his nickname by school friends impressed by his skill as a drummer, after the noted 1950s jazz drummer Cozy Cole, who played with Cab Calloway and Louis Armstrong.

Puff Daddy

Puff Daddy was born Sean Combs, and acquired the nickname "Puffy" from his habit of puffing out his chest while playing on the high school football team. He has recently changed his stage name to P-Diddy in the process of re-inventing his image.

Leo Sayer

Leo Sayer's real name is Gerard Hugh Sayer, and he was nicknamed "Leo" by Jackie, the wife of his manager, Adam Faith, because of his leonine mane of curly hair.

Boz Scaggs

Boz Scaggs was born William Royce Scaggs. Boz is short for "Bosley", a childhood nickname he picked up after a schoolmate, Donald Ivert, kept addressing him by that name.

Simply Red

Simply Red's lead singer Mick Hucknall is nicknamed "Red" owing to his red hair, and originally wanted to name the band Red also. After deciding that the name should be expanded and experimenting with several alternatives, Simply Red was eventually chosen. Another less likely story suggests the name came from an MC who, when asking how to introduce Hucknall (at that time performing solo), was told "Just Red...Simply Red".

Snoop Doggy Dogg

Snoop Doggy Dogg was born Calvin Broadus, and was nicknamed "Snoopy" by his mother because she thought he looked like the Peanuts comic strip character. As his cousin was nicknamed Tate Doggy Dogg, he took his stage name as a combination of both nicknames. After changing record labels, he abbreviated his name to Snoop Dogg.

Sting

Born Gordon Matthew Sumner, he was nicknamed Sting while playing with a dixieland jazz band called The Phoenix Jazzmen. Sting turned up to rehearsal one day wearing a hooped soccer jersey and his bandmate, trombone player Gordon Solomon, offered that he looked like a bee. From there, he became "Stinger", which eventually got shortened to Sting.

Tone Loc

Born Anthony Terrell Smith, his stage name is a shortened version of his Spanish nickname, Antonio Loco, meaning "Crazy Anthony".

Tricky

Adrian Thaws was nicknamed "Tricky Kid" while part of a teenage street gang, later shortening the nickname and adopting it as his stage name.

Midge Ure

Born James Ure but known as Jim, he arrived at his stage name by reversing the letters of his first name to spell "Mij", later modified to Midge.

Junior Walker

Junior Walker was born Oscar G. Mixon, but at some point in his childhood his name was changed to Autry DeWalt Jr. "Junior" was a childhood nickname, and it is thought that he took the name Walker from his stepfather. The backing group's name, The All-Stars, came from an audience comment about the band.

Zucchero

Born Adelmo Fornaciari, he was called "zucchero e marmellata" (Italian for "sugar and jam") by his primary school teacher, subsequently adopting the shortened version as his stage name.

Kith And Kin

Bands and artists whose names were
inspired by friends and family

Tori Amos

Born Myra Ellen Amos, for a while she was called Sammy Jayye in honor of the TV character Sammy Jo from the TV show *Dynasty* (played by Heather Locklear), which she was a big fan of. After telling the boyfriend of her friend Linda that she had been trying to think of a name for nine months, he suggested the name "Tori". She fronted a band called Y Kant Tori Read before going solo.

Animals

Initially known as The Alan Price Combo after keyboards player Alan Price, the original PR story was that they changed their name to The Animals, as it was more suited to their wild stage act. However, this is not true–vocalist Eric Burdon had initially suggested the name Animal Hogg and the Squatters in a pub brainstorming session, which came from a local (Newcastle) anarchic character called Jackie "Animal" Hogg, an Army veteran.

Atomic Rooster

An American band called Rhinoceros had a bass player called Peter Hodgson, who used to dress up in a rooster costume. He once proclaimed that he was ready to declare his identity to the world by shouting, "Yes! The Atomic Rooster!" Hodgson was later committed to a mental institution. Some sources claim the name was from an album title by Rhinoceros, but the only album title remotely close in Rhinoceros's discography is *Satin Chickens* (1969), so this is unlikely. Atomic Rooster's keyboards player Vincent Crane (*b.* Vincent Rodney Cheesman) met the band Rhinoceros and learned of the Atomic Rooster while in New York with The Crazy World of Arthur Brown.

Lavern Baker

Lavern Baker was born Delores Williams. Her early singing career saw her billed as "Little Miss Sharecropper" and also "Bea Baker", before finally adopting the name Lavern Baker while singing with Todd Rhodes and his Orchestra. Baker is a family name–she has an aunt called Merline Baker.

Bee Gees

A DJ called Bill Gates discovered the band as teenagers in Brisbane, Australia, when they were performing at a racetrack. They also met a racing driver at the same time called Bill Good, and both Good and Gates went home to meet the boy's parents. Gates pointed out that there were so many BGs in the room (Brothers Gibb, Barry Gibb, Bill Gates, Bill Good) that they should call themselves The BGs, which was later extended to The Bee Gees. In 1974, they officially dropped the prefix "The" and became simply Bee Gees.

Blind Melon

After considering several other names, including Brown Cow and The Naked Pilgrims, bass player Brad Smith walked in one day and said, "What's happening, blind melons?". That was how his dad used to greet the hippies who lived next door to them in Mississippi.

Captain Beefheart's Magic Band

Captain Beefheart was christened Don Van Vliet. A school friend of **Frank Zappa**, he took his stage name from Zappa's movie entitled *Captain Beefheart Meets the Grunt People*. Zappa later emphasized the appropriateness of the name by saying that Beefheart "had a beef in his heart against the world".

Richard Clayderman

Born Phillipe Pages, he changed his name from Pages (pronounced "parje") to avoid mispronunciation, adopting his Swedish great-grandmother's name.

Elvis Costello

Elvis Costello was born Declan Patrick McManus, starting his career with the stage name D.P. Costello, Costello being his paternal great-grandmother's maiden name. The name Elvis was suggested by Costello's manager Jake Riviera (*b.* Andrew Jakeman), basically to annoy people. He had earlier formed a band called Flip City, from a comment made by Cheech Marin on Joni Mitchell's album *Court And Spark* (1974).

Crowded House

Originally called the Mullanes, after lead singer Neil Finn's middle name, their new name was a reference to the open-door policy at their Hollywood rented accommodation, into which bass player Nick Seymour especially was constantly inviting people round.

Crystals

The Crystals would often rehearse at songwriter Leroy Bates's sister-in-law's house because she had a piano, and they took their name as a tribute to Bates' baby daughter, Crystal.

Vic Damone

Born Vito Rocco Farinola, he started performing as Vic Farinola, and then decided to change his name to Vic Damone while on the way to his first professional singing job at New York radio station WHN. Damone was his mother's maiden name.

Chris De Burgh

Chris De Burgh was born Christopher John Davidson, adopting his mother's maiden name as his stage name when he became a performer.

Fun Loving Criminals

This name comes from a Queens, New York graffiti crew, called Fun Lovin' Crime, run by a friend of the band, and represents the difficulty of living in New York, where it is hard to stay on the right side of the law. Huey (guitar–*b.* Huey Morgan); Fast (bass), *AKA* Fisty, was born Brian Leiser, and acquired his nickname from his lackadaisical attitude to answering phones at The Limelight Club in New York.

Billie Holiday

Billie Holiday was born Eleanora Fagan Gough. She took the last part of her stage name from her father Clarence Holiday (her parent's were never married) and her first name from the silent-movie star Billie Dove, *AKA* "The American Beauty" after the title of one of her movies, whom Holiday admired.

Hootie & The Blowfish

Lead vocalist Darius Rucker played in a college show choir called "Carolina Alive" with Ervin Harris, who was nicknamed "Hootie" for his owlish glasses, and Donald Feaster, nicknamed "The Blowfish" because of his puffy cheeks. One day they walked into a room together and Rucker exclaimed "Its Hootie and The Blowfish!".

Janis Ian

Born Janis Eddy Fink, she had initially wanted to call herself Jasmine Thompson. Ian was her brother's middle name and she started using it as her last name when she was 13. She titled her third album *The Secret Life Of J. Eddy Fink* (1968), referring to her real name.

Jane's Addiction

Jane's Addiction was named in reference to a friend of band members Perry Farrell and Eric Avery called Jane Bainter, who had a heroin problem. Perry Farrell (vocals–b. Perry Bernstein–the name Farrell is a play on the word "peripheral").

Elton John

Elton John was born Reginald Kenneth Dwight. He took his stage name in tribute to sax player Elton Dean and vocalist and friend **Long John Baldry**, both of whom he played with in the band Bluesology. The full version of his stage name is actually Elton Hercules John, Hercules being the name of the horse owned by the main characters in BBC TV sitcom Steptoe and Son (re-made in the US as Sanford and Son).

Al Jolson

Born Asa Yoelson in Lithuania before moving to the US with his family, he changed his name to Al following the example set by his brother Hirsch, who had anglicized his first name by changing it to Harry. He changed the spelling of his last name, first to Joelson then to Jolson, when he began a comedy act with his brother.

Gladys Knight & The Pips

The group was initially formed as The Pips, inspired by their cousin and manager's nickname, James "Pip" Woods. They were later re-named Gladys Knight & The Pips when Knight moved to the forefront.

Limmie & The Family Cookin'

This group's name was taken from leader Limmie Frank Snell, with the "Family Cookin'" part taken from the fact that the other group members were his siblings, Jimmy and Martha.

Limp Bizkit

The name Limp Bizkit was inspired during a conversation between vocalist Fred Durst and a friend (now a roadie with the band), when the phrase "brain like a limp biscuit" was used in respect of the effects of overindulgence in pot smoking.

Nico

Nico was born Christa Päffgen, and her stage name was suggested by a photographer in honor of his friend, film-maker Nico Papatakis.

NSync

Group member Justin Timberlake's mother Lynn Harless came up with this name, which is made up of the last letters of the group members' names:- JustiN (Justin Timberlake), ChriS (Chris Kirkpatrick), JoeY (Joey Fatone), LansteN (James Lansten "Lance" Bass) and JC (short for Joshua Chasez).

O'Jays

Originally known as The Mascots, they changed their name to The O'Jays in tribute to Cleveland DJ, Eddie O'Jay, who championed their early record releases on radio. Their first record producer Don Davis claimed he told them to switch names.

Pearl Jam

Initially called Mookie Blaylock after the NBA star of that name (and whose jersey number gave them the name of their debut album, *Ten* (1991)), Pearl Jam took their new name after a hallucinogenic preserve made by vocalist Eddie Vedder's great grandmother Pearl, who was married to an Indian chief. Vedder was born Edward Louis Severson III, Vedder being his mother's maiden name. His birth name is sometimes given as Mueller, however this is the name of the man (Peter Mueller) who married his mother and adopted him.

Pet Shop Boys

The Pet Shop Boys were originally known as West End, after the district of London where they were living. Keyboards player Chris Lowe had three friends who worked at the same pet store in Ealing in west London, and Lowe and vocalist Neil Tennant would suggest to them that they start a band called The Pet Shop Boys. When West End decided to change their name they decided instead to use the name for themselves.

Pink Fairies

The Pink Fairies took their name from a London drinking club set up by future leader Mick Farren (then with The Deviants), Steve Took of Tyrannosaurus Rex and ex-Pretty Things member Twink (b. John C. Alder). The club was called The Pink Fairies Motorcycle Club and All-Star Rock and Roll Band.

P J Proby

P J Proby was born James Marcus Smith. His original stage name was Jeff Powers, so chosen because Jim Smith was considered too plain for the stage. His final stage name was suggested by his friend and noted songwriter, Sharon Sheeley, PJ Proby being the name of an ex-boyfriend of hers from San Diego.

Del Shannon

Del Shannon was born Charles Weedon Westover. He joined a band at the Hi-Lo Club in Battle Creek, Michigan where a regular told him of his dreams of becoming a pro-wrestler using the name "Mark Shannon". Westover liked the name Shannon and decided to use it himself. He arrived at his first name Del from a contraction of the name of his favorite car, the DeVille (Cadillac Coupe DeVille).

Wee Papa Girl Rappers

Sisters TV Tim (b. Timmie Lawrence) and Total S (b. Sandra Lawrence) took their group name from "Wee Papa!", a phrase their father would exclaim when excited.

Kim Wilde

Kim Wilde, who is the daughter of **Marty Wilde** (*b.* Reginald Smith), was born Kim Smith.

Hometown Favorites

Bands and artists whose names were
inspired by their hometown region

Alabama

The band were made up of cousins from Fort Payne, Alabama and, after initially being known as Young Country and then Wild Country, they finally settled on the name of their home state.

All Saints

Group members Melanie Blatt (named after folk singer Melanie) and Shaznay Lewis first came together doing session work at Metamorphosis Studios on All Saints Road in London's Notting Hill, and when they formed their own band they decided to use the studio's location as their name.

Area Code 615

Area Code 615 were a group of Nashville-based session men who were brought together initially to make only one album, taking their name from the local metropolitan area dialing code.

Atlanta Rhythm Section

The Atlanta Rhythm Section was formed by a group of session musicians who were the house band at Studio One in Doraville, near Atlanta, Georgia. They adopted the name of the city when they decided to become a full-time band.

Backstreet Boys

The Backstreet Boys were originally named The Backstreet Market after a famous open-air market in Orlando, Florida that was a local teen hangout, later changing to Backstreet Boys.

Big Star

This name was taken from the name of a supermarket across the street from their recording studio, Ardent Studios in Memphis, Tennessee–Big Star Foodmakers is a supermarket chain in Memphis.

Black Oak Arkansas

Black Oak Arkansas was formed originally as The Knowbody Else, taking their new name from the birthplace of the band's leader, Jim "Jim Dandy" Mangrum.

Boston

The group formed in Boston, Massachussetts and was named after the city at the suggestion of their record producer, John Boylan.

Bush

Bush was named after the Shepherds Bush area of London, close to where they lived. They were initially formed as Future Primitive, and were allegedly asked to change to a shorter name for cost purposes.

Champaign

This group originated in and took as their stage name the name of their home city, Champaign, Illinois.

Chi-Lites

Named Marshall & the Hi-Lites for their drummer Marshall Thompson, the group then changed to Marshall & the Chi-Lites, referring to their Chicago origins, following the discovery of an existing group called The Hi-Lites. They later trimmed the name to The Chi-Lites.

Coasters

The Coasters were formed originally as The Robins in Los Angeles, and when they signed to Atlantic Records, the record company wanted to take them to New York to record. Some of them stayed behind as The Robins, while the others changed their name to The Coasters in tribute to their West Coast origins.

Cockney Rebel

Vocalist Steve Harley was born Steven Nice in South London, where the locals are known as Cockneys. He changed his last name to "Harley" as it sounded a lot tougher than "Nice".

Cypress Hill

Cypress Hill started out as DVX (Devastating Vocal Excellence), but changed their name when original member Method Man Ace (b. Ulpiano Sergio Reyes, Sen Dog's younger brother) quit for a solo career. The name Cypress Hill comes from a street (Cypress Avenue, where Sen Dog had lived) in South Central Los Angeles. The member's nicknames are Sen Dog (b. Senen Reyes), B-Real (b. Louis Freese), Muggs (b. Lawrence Muggerud).

Marcella Detroit

Marcella Detroit was born Marcy Levy in Detroit, Michigan and, although already successful, adopted the name of her hometown as her stage name when she formed the duo **Shakespear's Sister** with Siobhan Fahey, previously of **Bananarama**.

Detroit Spinners

Originally formed as The Domingoes, The Spinners (as they were known in the US) added the prefix "Detroit" for the UK market, in order to avoid confusion with the British folk group of the same name.

Diesel Park West

This name is a reference to the location of their recording studio, situated in the middle of a diesel truck park. The band was originally called The Filberts, after Filbert Street, the home ground of Leicester City F.C., the soccer team whichh plays in Leicester, the town in which they were formed.

Dion & The Belmonts

Dion was born Dion Di Mucci, and the group took its name from Belmont Avenue, a street in their hometown Bronx, New York neighborhood.

Dru Hill

Dru Hill was named after the Baltimore neighborhood in which they formed, Druid Hill Park. The members included: Jazz (b. Larry Anthony Jr) is a jazz fan; Sisqo (b. Mark Andrews); Nokio (b. Tamir Ruffin)–NOKIO stands for Nasty On Key In Octave; Woody (b. James Green) is nicknamed after his grandfather, Woodrow.

Dubliners

The Dubliners were formed in O'Donoghue's Bar in Merron Row,Dublin, taking their name in honor of their hometown. They were originally named The Ronnie Drew Group, after their founder member.

East 17

This band originally formed as E17, which is the postal code of Walthamstow, their hometown borough of London. They later expanded the name to East 17 to distance themselves from the drug ecstasy, commonly known as "e".

Everything But The Girl

Everything But The Girl was the name of a furniture shop in the northern English town of Hull, often reported unfairly as being a second-hand store. In fact, it sold new (but out-dated) furniture, and, indeed, it was often said that "everything but the girl" (assistant) was for sale.

Fairport Convention

Fairport Convention took their name from "Fairport", the name of band member Simon Nicol's home in Muswell Hill, London, where they used to rehearse.

Fatima Mansions

Fatima Mansions named themselves after a run-down housing estate in Dublin, Ireland, where band leader Cathal Coughlan was raised. The trend in Dublin at that time was to give names with religious themes to new housing projects, this particular estate being named for the Catholic shrine at Fatima, in Portugal, where the Virgin Mary allegedly appeared to a group of children in 1917.

Tennessee Ernie Ford

Born Ernest Jennings Ford, in Bristol, Tennessee, he first picked up the nickname "Tennessee Ernie" while deejaying for KXFM in San Bernandino, CA. He would use the name Tennessee Ernie Ford for the hillbilly slot, switching to his given name of Ernest Ford for more serious announcing.

Gap Band

This name is made up from the initial letters of 3 streets, Greenwood, Archer and Pine, which formed the African-American business center of their hometown of Tulsa, Oklahoma. Originally they were known as The Greenwood Archer Pine Street Band, later shortening to the G.A.P. Band, and finally becoming The Gap Band after a typo omitted the periods.

Geordie

Citizens of Newcastle-upon-Tyne, UK (where the band was formed, and incidentally home to the finest soccer team in the world) are known as "Geordies". The term originated during the Jacobite rebellion in 18th-century Britain, where people loyal to King George were known as "Geordies", a distortion of the King's name.

Georgia Satellites

The Georgia Satellites were an Atlanta, Georgia-based band, taking their name from their home state. They were originally named by drummer David Michaelson as Keith & the Satellites (after bass player Keith Christopher), then changed to the Satellites, and finally Georgia Satellites.

Hollywood Argyles

The name Hollywood Argyles was created for a one-off recording by vocalist Gary Paxton, who was already in another band, Skip and Flip, and who therefore could not be identified for contractual reasons. The group name came from a local intersection, Hollywood Boulevard and

Argyle Street, close to their studio, American Recording Studios, and was suggested by Paxton.

Johnny & The Hurricanes

Johnny & The Huricanes took the first part of their name from their sax player Johnny Paris (b. John Pocisk). As they came from Ohio, they adopted the group name "Hurricanes" because hurricanes and tornadoes are a regular occurrence in that part of the States at certain times of the year.

Kansas

The lineup of Kansas that achieved success was actually the third version of the band to use that name. Initially revolving around members who had been high school friends in the Kansas town of Topeka, the first two lineups who used the name Kansas disbanded and various members reformed as White Clover, which is a wildflower common in Kansas. They later once again adopted the name of their home state on recruiting guitarist Kerry Livgren, after their record company expressed their dislike of the name White Clover.

Kraftwerk

"Kraftwerk" is German for "power station", and the band decided to use that name because their first recording studio (Connie Plank's) was located in the middle of an oil refinery.

La's

The La's hailed from Liverpool, in England, where the word "la's" is local vernacular for "lads". The band was named by original frontman Mike Badger, who says the name came to him in a dream.

Leyton Buzzards

This group formed in Leyton in East London, and derived their name by mixing the name of their hometown with that of another, similarly-named town in the south-west of England, Leighton Buzzard.

Linkin Park

Linkin Park started life as Xero, before adopting the name Hybrid Theory (which was later used as the name of their first album recorded under the name Linkin Park). They chose their final name as a deliberately misspelt version of the Santa Monica, California landmark, Lincoln Park, an idea suggested by vocalist Chester Bennington. References quote that the spelling was changed to make the registration of the Web site easier, however the domain name <lincolnpark.com> was available at the time of this book going to press, so this seems unlikely.

MC5

The MC5 originally formed as The Motor City 5 in Detroit (coincidentally in a place called Lincoln Park–see above entry), "Motor City" being a nickname for Detroit in honor of its many automobile plants (which fact also christened the record label Motown, short for "Motor Town"). Robin "Rob" Tyner was born Robert Derminer and borrorowed his last name from jazz pianist McCoy Tyner. Wayne Kramer (b. Wayne Kambes) was renamed by bandmate Tyner, who also invented the nicknames of band mates Fred "Sonic" Smith and Dennis "Machine Gun" Thompson.

Merseybeats

The Merseybeats formed in Liverpool, the home of the so-called Mersey Sound of the 1960s–the Mersey being the name of a river that runs through Liverpool.

Mighty Mighty Bosstones

The Mighty Mighty Bosstones were originally formed as The Bosstones, which name was inspired by their home-town of Boston. After discovering that a 1950s Harvard accapella group called The Bosstones had previously existed, they added the prefix "Mighty Mighty" thanks to a suggestion by a bartender friend.

Ohio Players

Formed in Dayton, Ohio as an R&B backing band and originally called The Ohio Untouchables, they changed their name on the departure of guitarist Robert Ward, in reference to their instrumental prowess.

Paper Lace

Paper Lace took their name in honor of the lace industry for which their home town of Nottingham, UK, has been famous for more than 200 years.

Portishead

Portishead are named after a suburb in Bristol in the UK, where leader Geoff Barrow was living at the time. When he first began recording, he was dubbed "that guy from Portishead" which led to the idea for the band name.

Johnny Rivers

Johnny Rivers was born John Henry Ramistella, and was re-named at the suggestion of rock 'n' roll DJ Alan Freed.

When Rivers, Freed and Freed's manager Jack Hooke were sitting around discussing what name to use, Rivers mentioned how he had grown up close to the Mississippi River and his stage name developed from that.

Roxy Music

Originally named by Brian Ferry after a local cinema (Roxy), they later added the suffix "Music" to differentiate themselves from a similarly-named American band. Phil Manzanera (guitars) was born Philip Targett-Adams, but chose to use his Colombian-born mother's maiden name for the stage.

Sham 69

The name Sham 69 was inspired by graffiti seen on a wall in Hersham, near London, where the band was formed, reading "Hersham 69".

Southside Johnny & The Asbury Jukes

Southside Johnny (b. John Lyon) took his stage name from Chicago's Southside, where the famous blues clubs are situated. The name was a compromise between the original suggestion of Chicago Johnny, made by his Asbury Park contemporary, Bruce Springsteen, and his own counter-suggestion of Chicago Southside. The Asbury Jukes formed out of The Blackberry Booze Band in Asbury Park, New Jersey.

Strawbs

The Strawbs started life as a bluegrass group, The Strawberry Hill Boys, a name invented on the spot by founder member Dave Cousins. Asked for their name just as they were about to go on at their first gig, he replied "The Strawberry Hill Boys". Strawberry Hill is an area in the

Twickenham district of London where they used to rehearse. This was shortened to Strawbs the year after their
formation.

Global Village

Bands and artists whose names were
inspired by a particular place

Lionel Bart

Oliver composer Lionel Bart was born Lionel Begleiter in Stepney, London. Unhappy with his given last name, he changed it to Bart after seeing St Bartholomew's hospital (known as St. Bart's) in East London, while riding by on a bus.

Beautiful South

The Beautiful South were formed in the northern English port town of Hull. Their name is a sarcastic reference to the view of their previous band **The Housemartins** as dour northerners, a perception fueled by the traditional rivalry that exists in England between the largely blue-collar, working-class north and the more white-collar, middle-class south.

Booker T & the MGs

The MGs began life as the house band for Stax Records, the name being made up of part of leader Booker T. Jones' name, with MG standing for "Memphis Group", in honor of the city where they were formed.

Brownsville Station

This name is famous as the name of the southernmost city of the USA (in Texas). Leader Michael Koda took the nickname "Cub" from Carl "Cubby" O'Brien, a Mouseketeer of the Mickey Mouse Club.

John Denver

John Denver was born Henry John Deuetschendorf, and decided to change his name when he moved to LA in the

'60s to be part of the music scene there. Friends suggested that he use the name John Sommerville, but instead he took the name of the capital city (Denver) of his home state, Colorado.

Easterhouse

A staunch left-wing political band, Easterhouse were formed in Manchester, UK and took their name from a Glasgow, Scotland working-class housing estate, developed in the 1950s, which became synonymous with social depravation, poverty and high unemployment.

Europe

Originally named The Force, they changed to Europe to reflect their Swedish roots by band member Joey Tempest. Tempest was born Joakim Larsson, and took his stage name from Shakespeare's last play, *The Tempest*.

Four Seasons

Originally The Four Lovers, they changed their name to that of a bowling alley in Union, New Jersey after they had an unsuccessful audition there, in order that they would at least leave the audition with something. Frankie Valli (b. Francis Stephen Castelluccio) first recorded as Frankie Valley, having seen country star Jean Valley performing when he was a child.

Grand Funk Railroad

Grand Funk Railroad were formed in Flint, Michigan and took their name from a Michigan landmark, the Grand Trunk Western Railroad, part of the Canadian National Railway.

Hatfield & The North

A London band, they took their name from a road sign–"Hatfield & The North"–the first road sign seen on the M1 motorway leaving London. The name was suggested by Mike Patto, a friend of the band.

Lindisfarne

A band from Newcastle, in the northeast of England, Lindisfarne were originally formed as Downtown Faction before changing their name to Brethren. After discovering that the name "Brethren" was already being used by an American band, they took their final name from the "holy island" of Lindisfarne, site of an ancient Christian monastery off the coast of Northumbria, England, close to where they were formed.

Little River Band

An Australian band, they started out as Mississippi, but this American-sounding name was not popular with their more ardent fans. Glenn Shorrock suggested their new name when they drove by a sign for the small town of Little River near Geelong, Victoria, at first thinking that it would make a good song title.

M

The name M was inspired by the signs for the Paris Metro (subway), which appear as a large yellow "M" within a circle.

Notting Hillbillies

The Notting Hillbillies was a group put together by **Dire Straits** guitarist Mark Knopfler and his longtime friends

Brendan Croker and Steve Phillips, initially as a hobby band, one night in a wine bar in London's Notting Hill. Three years after their first pub gigs the band eventually recorded an album.

Oasis

Oasis were named after the Swindon Oasis, a leisure center venue in Swindon, UK, which was seen by vocalist Liam Gallagher as a gig date on an **Inspiral Carpets** poster, brother Noel having been a roadie with the band.

Power Station

An offshoot project for Robert Palmer and members of **Duran Duran**, Power Station was named after the New York recording studio in which they recorded–now called Avatar Studios.

Rainbow

Rainbow were named after the Rainbow Bar & Grill on Sunset Boulevard, Los Angeles, where Ritchie Blackmore and members of the band Elf, later to join with him to form Rainbow, used to hang out. The band used the name Ritchie Blackmore's Rainbow on their first album.

Rutles

A spoof band, The Rutles was a spinoff from the UK TV series Rutland Weekend Television, and was a clever pastiche of the **Beatles**. They did eventually make an album. Rutland was at the time England's smallest county and the butt of many jokes, although it lost its county status and was absorbed into Leicestershire in 1974. After a long campaign, Rutland regained its status as a county in 1997.

SOS Band

The SOS Band was formed originally in Atlanta, Georgia under the name Sounds Of Santa Monica, so-called because they had at one time enjoyed a particularly successful gig in Santa Monica, California. This was later abbreviated to SOS Band at the suggestion of their producer Sigidi Adullah, with the initials SOS now representing "Sounds Of Success".

Spandau Ballet

Starting out as The Makers, they changed their name to Spandau Ballet at the suggestion of BBC broadcaster Bob Elms. Elms had seen the phrase written on a toilet wall in Berlin, where Spandau was the name of the prison famous for holding a solitary prisoner, Nazi war criminal Rudolph Hess.

Tom Tom Club

An offshoot project of **Talking Heads**, Tom Tom Club recorded their first album in the Bahamas, and took their name from that of their rehearsal hall.

Conway Twitty

Conway Twitty was born Harold Lloyd Jenkins, named after the silent movie star Harold Lloyd. After being urged to adopt a stage name by his producer, he spent some time studying a map and chose "Conway" in Arkansas and "Twitty" in Texas.

Village People

The Village People were put together by French disco producer Jacques Morali after seeing groups of gay men in Greenwich Village dancing together in costume.

Traditional

Bands and artists whose names were inspired
by an aspect of history or mythology

A3

The band's full name is Alabama 3, and is a reference to the Alabama 2, victims of a lynch-mob administering summary southern white justice in 1930's America, the members being heavily involved with organizations such as Miscarriages of Justice. The band is known as A3 in the US after objections to the use of their full name from country band **Alabama**. The band members have adopted the surname "Love"–Very Reverend Dr D. Wayne Love (real name Jake Black), Larry Love (real name Robert Spragg).

Apollo 440

This band's name has two inspirations, taking Apollo from the Greek god of music, and the number 440 from the name of the sequencer/sampler they were using–a Sequential Studio 440, and not from the frequency of the "A" note as is sometimes reported.

Art Of Noise

The Art Of Noise were so-named by lyricist Paul Morley after a futurist manifesto (*Art Of Noises*), published in 1913 by Italian Luigi Russolo. He made "intonorumori" or "noise machines", and wrote music for them. When Morley heard the kinds of sounds the as-yet unnamed band was producing, he decided to name them "Art of Noises", later dropping the "s".

Bauhaus

Bauhaus was formed as Bauhaus 1919, a name suggested by band member David Jay (*AKA* David J, *b.* David Jay Haskins) and taken from the German art and design school, Das Bauhaus. The Bauhaus was first set up in 1919 in Weimar, and its "less is more" credo was in keeping with the band's minimalist approach to music. After recording a couple of demos, the band dropped the suffix "1919" from their name.

Belle Stars

Guitarist Sarah-Jane Owen wore cowgirl fashions, and the term "belle star" is used to describe American cowgirls. The term originally came from Belle Starr (b. Myra Belle Shirley, she later married Sam Starr), a famous American female horse-thief in the mid-1800s.

David Bowie

David Bowie was born David Robert Hayward-Jones, changing his name for the stage while with R&B band The Lower Third, at the suggestion of **Manfred Mann**'s manager Kenneth Pitt. Pitt, who would later go on to become Bowie's manager, had suggested the name change to avoid confusion with Davy Jones, lead singer with the **Monkees**. He took the last name "Bowie" from the knife invented by Col. Sam Bowie. Earlier in his career he played with The Mannish Boys, named after the **Muddy Waters'** classic, "Mannish Boy".

Cabaret Voltaire

Cabaret Voltaire were named after the café in Zurich which was established in 1916 and used by Swiss Dadaists to hold their meetings. The band identified with certain aspects of the Dadaist movement, a loose group of western European artists and writers seeking the abolition of traditional cultural forms, in reaction to the music establishment at the time they were formed.

Communards

The Communards initially formed as The Committee, but after the discovery that a band with that name already existed they adopted the name Communards as a reflection of their ideological beliefs. "Communards" was the name given to the people of Paris who set up a provisional government called the Commune, following the Franco-Prussian war (1870–1).

Country Joe & The Fish

The name Country Joe is attributed to leader, Joe McDonald. The original suggestion for the band name was made by their manager Ed Denson as "Country Mao and the Fish", from a quote by Mao-Tse Tung that "people are like water, and the army is like fish", from *Aspects of China's Anti-Japanese Struggle* (1948). However, the band didn't like "Country Mao" and changed it to Country Joe and The Fish.

Durutti Column

A 1960s European anarchist group, the Situationists Internationale, papered the walls of Strasbourg in 1966 with a comic strip entitled "The Return of the Durutti Column", inspired by Spanish Civil War revolutionary Buenaventura Durruti (note the different spelling). The band took the name at the suggestion of manager Tony Wilson of Factory Records fame.

Fields Of The Nephilim

The Nephilim are referenced in the Book of Genesis and are assumed from the text to be the offspring of angels and humans, although all references to the Nephilim were removed from the Bible by the Catholic Council. The band chose "Nephilim" because they are mysterious and nobody knows much about them (thanks largely to the Catholic Council), adding "Fields" to represent magnetic fields pulling in towards the Nephilim.

Filter

Filter took their name from a concept developed by 18th-century philosopher Immanuel Kant in his work, *The Critique of Pure Reason* (1781), wherein the mind acts as a cultural filter to organize our perception of reality.

Foo Fighters

"Foo Fighters" was a term used by US pilots in the Second World War to describe apparent UFOs, supposedly of German origin and known colloquially as "Kraut Balls". The word 'foo' is an Anglicization of 'feu', the French word for 'fire'. Dave Grohl, leader of the group, chose the name because he is an avid sci-fi fan, to such an extent that he appeared as an extra in an episode of *The X-Files*. In 1935, a comic strip character called Smokey Stover appeared in the *Chicago Tribune*, created by Bill Holman–the character was a fireman, but referred to himself as a "foofighter", and this may have influenced the use of the term during the war.

Freznal Rhomb

Freznal Rhomb named themselves after lead vocalist Jason Whalley's rat, which in turn had been named for a device (the Fresnel Rhomb) invented by French scientist Augustus Fresnel.

Gang Of Four

A four-piece with strong political views, they took their name from the Chinese revolutionaries of the late '70s led by Madame Jiang Qing.

Go West

This name comes from the phrase "Go West, young man!", used in a newspaper article written by John Soule, an Indiana newspaperman, in 1851, although the article appeared some ten years after Horace Greeley in the *New Yorker* had urged people to head out West to seek their fortune.

Gryphon

Playing everything from early pre-classical music to rock, Gryphon were named after a mythical animal composed of parts of other animals, which represented their own hybrid of musical tastes.

James Gang

The James Gang took their name from the legendary Wild West outlaw gang, which included the infamous Jesse James.

Jars Of Clay

A Christian band, this name comes from a line in the *Bible* (II Corinthians 4.7) written by the Apostle Paul: "But we have this treasure in jars of clay [or "earthen vessels", depending on which version of the Bible is referred] to show that this all-surpassing power is from God and not from us". The band wanted a name which would remind them to be humble, and the source is explained on the track "Four Seven" (a reference to the verse number from the album *Jars Of Clay* (1995).

Jethro Tull

Jethro Tull were named after the 18th-century English agriculturalist who invented the seed drill. They were in the habit of changing their name regularly, but at the time the name Jethro Tull was suggested by their agent (who had been a history student in college) they were offered a residency at London's Marquee Club, so that name became their final choice.

Johnny Kidd & The Pirates

Leader Johhny Kidd (*b.* Frederick Heath) started wearing an eyepatch after a guitar string accident, leading to EMI recording engineer Peter Sullivan dubbing his band Johnny Kidd & The Pirates. Captain (William) Kidd was a notorious 17th-century English pirate.

Justified Ancients Of Mu-Mu

The Justified Ancients of Mu-Mu was a **KLF** project, the name being taken from a secret society in the conspiracy novels by Robert Shea and Robert Anton Wilson, dealing with the *Illuminati*. The Illuminati were originally an 18th-century group of conspirators financed by international bankers. The name of the project was chosen because KLF band member Bill Drummond had helped put on a stage play called "Illuminatus!", based on the cult book trilogy, while attending art college.

Levellers

The Levellers were English Civil War activists in the 17th-century, whose intent was to 'level' the monarchy to be equal to the common people. The band chose this name as being representative of their ideas on contemporary social issues.

Molly Hatchet

Molly Hatchet was one of 18 names put into a hat to choose a name for the band. The name was based on the name of a prostitute, dubbed in the press as Hatchet Molly, who terrorized 17th-century Salem by dispatching her clients with a meat cleaver.

New Christy Minstrels

The New Christy Minstrels were named after a famous American 19th-century minstrel show, "Christy's Minstrels", itself named for founder Edwin Pearce "Pops" Christy.

New Model Army

New Model Army were named after the Cromwellian parliamentary army in the Civil War of 1642, and chose the name as it had been the closest thing to a revolutionary army in England's history. The band was unaware of the subsequent oppression of the Irish by Cromwell's army at the time they picked the name.

Gary Puckett & The Union Gap

Vocalist Gary Puckett was an American Civil War buff and, although he was born in Minnesota, his family subsequently moved and he was raised in Yakima, close to the scene of a great battle at Union Gap, Washington. The band took their name from this historic town and dressed on stage in Civil War outfits.

Spear Of Destiny

"Spear of Destiny" is one of the names applied to the weapon which pierced Christ's side while on the cross. It was said to have been wielded by the Roman centurion Longinus and allegedly used and coveted by world leaders throughout history, including Hitler, because of its magical powers.

Styx

So-named after the mythological River Styx, the underworld river of Greek mythology separating the world of the living from that of the dead, which the souls of dead people have to cross over. Keyboard player Dennis De Young was a teacher at the time, and Dante's *Inferno* was being taught in Music Appreciation.

Troggs

Student hitchhikers originally suggested the name "The Grotty Trogs", later adopted by the band as The Troglodytes (a "troglodyte" is a prehistoric cave-dweller), before shortening the name again to The Troggs. Reg Presley (vocals–*b.* Reginald Ball); Ronnie Bond (drums–*b.* Ronnie Bullis).

Wu-Tang Clan

The Wu-Tang Clan were named for the rebels (experts in the art fighting with the Wu-Tang sword) who sought to overthrow the Shaolin temple. This was inspired by the band members' love of Chinese martial arts films. Method Man (*b.* Clifford Smith) took his name from a kind of marijuana known locally as "Method"; Ol' Dirty Bastard (*b.*

Russell Tyrone Jones); Ghostface Killah (*b*. Dennis Coles); The RZA (*b*. Robert F Diggs); The GZA (*b*. Gary Grice)– "GZA" is apparently the sound made when scratching out his previous alter-ego "Genius" on a record; Raekwon the Chef (*b*. Corey Woods)–"CHEF" stands for Criminals Have to Eat Food"; Inspectah Deck (*b*. Jason Hunter); U God (*b*. Lamont Hawkins), Masta Killa (*b*. Jamal Turner); Cappadonna (*b*. Daryl Hill).

Culture Vultures

Bands and artists whose names were inspired
by an aspect of language or culture

Apache Indian

Born Steve Kapur of Indian parentage, his main musical influence was reggae, and he took his stage name from his hero, Jamaican dance hall reggae star, Wild Apache Supercat.

Aswad

A reggae band, Aswad took their name from the Aramaic (some references mention Arabic) word for "black". Drummie Zeb (drums–b. Angus Gaye).

Pato Banton

Born Patrick Murray, he was christened "Pato Banton" by his stepfather, after "Pato", a wise Jamaican owl named for it's sound ("patoo") and "banton", meaning "heavy-weight" in Jamaican DJ circles.

Bentley Rhythm Ace

This name comes from the band members' weekend habit of shopping for rare records at car boot sales, a Bentley being an up-market British make of car. Car boot sales are like garage sales, but items are (in theory at least) sold from the boot (trunk) of a car. They regularly incorporated samples from the records they bought at these sales into their own music. Members Michael Barrywoosh (b. Michael Stokes); Barry Island (b. Richard Marsh)–Barry Island is near Cardiff, Wales.

Bhundu Boys

"Bhundu" is Zimbabwean for "bush", and the group name was chosen because leader Biggie Tembo (born Rodwell Marasha) had been a "bhundu boy", an under age runner for the rebel soldiers, during Zimbabwe's struggle for liberation.

Big Brother & Holding Co.

The band had written a list of potential names which they asked their manager Chris Helms to look over. "Big Brother" was close to the top of the list and "The Holding Company" was close to the bottom; Helms suggested they combine the two names. "Holding" is a term used for possessing drugs.

Acker Bilk

Acker Bilk was born Bernard Stanley Bilk in Somerset in England, taking the first name "Acker" for the stage as it is a local slang term meaning "pal" or "mate".

Black Uhuru

This Jamaican reggae band was originally called Uhuru, taking their name from the Swahili word "uhuru", which means "freedom". They later extended the name to Black Uhuru, i.e. "Black Freedom".

Blow Monkeys

Lead vocalist Dr Robert (b. Bruce Robert Howard) picked up this term, which is slang for Aboriginal didgeridoo players, while growing up in Australia. Howard earned the nickname "Doctor" through being known as a sympathetic listener.

Blue Cheer

Blue Cheer were a 1960s heavy rock band who named themselves for a high-quality strain of LSD, which was itself named after a popular detergent.

Boo Yaa T.R.I.B.E.

A Samoan-American band whose members had been involved with street gangs, they took their name from the slang word "boo-yaa", which represents the sound of a shotgun blast. T.R.I.B.E. represents "Too Rough International Boo-Yaa Empire".

Chantays

The Chantays took their name from the French verb "chanter", meaning "to sing", although ironically their only hit was an instrumental ("Pipeline").

Clannad

"Clannad" is the Gaelic word for "family", and comes from the group comprising brothers, sisters (including **Enya**) and uncles from the Bhraonain and Dugain families (or Brennan and Duggan as anglicized). The group was initially known as "an clan as Dobhar", meaning "family from Dore".

Cornershop

Cornershop's name is an ironic comment on British anti-Asian racism, particularly the myth that every Asian family in Britain has a shop on a street corner.

Dana

Dana was born Rosemary Brown in Derry, Ireland, and her stage name is a Gaelic word meaning "bold" or "mischievous". She later discovered that Dana was a goddess giving her name to an ancient Irish tribe (Tuatha De Danann, literally "People of Dana"), who were skilled in the crafts.

Dexy's Midnight Runners

This name refers to Dexedrine, a pep pill widely used by all-night dancers during the "Northern Soul" era of the late 1960s and early '70s, when dance clubs in the north of England (most notably Wigan Casino) championed non-charting soul music.

Doobie Brothers

A doobie is a slang term for a marijuana cigarette (larger than a joint), the name being suggested by a friend of the band. The origin of the word "doobie" is unknown.

Einsturzende Neubauten

"Einsturzende Neubauten" is German and roughly translates as "New buildings collapsing", referring to the buildings erected in Germany after the Second World War which were so poorly constructed that they often collapsed.

Fixx

The Fixx formed originally as The Fix, a reference to drugs. Their record label, MCA, was uneasy about this, and insisted that they add the extra 'x'.

Flying Pickets

This acapella group formed out of the 7:84 Theatre Group, so-called because 7 per cent of the UK population were supposed to own 84 per cent of the wealth. They chose the name "Flying Pickets" as this represented their political motivation. Flying pickets are outsiders brought in to bolster picket lines during strikes, and are not necessarily directly related to the cause.

Gorky's Zygotic Mynci

A Welsh band, the name is a nonsense phrase of three unrelated words, and translates more-or-less phonetically from the Welsh as "Dimwit Reproductive Monkey"–the band has commented that, had they known they were going to be successful, they would have spent more time on thinking up a name.

Jesus Jones

This band's name took shape while they were on a Spanish beach, where several of the locals were named Jesus ("hay-soos"). It was felt that Jesus was as popular in the Spanish phone book as Jones was in the English version, so they married the two names together (although not using the Spanish pronunciation). Gen (drums–b. Simon Matthews) got his nickname after starting a new school, when he was given a hard time by the incumbent kids and always retorted with the exclamation "Genital!", later resulting in the abbreviated nickname.

Chaka Khan

Chaka Khan was born Yvette Marie Stevens, and was given her alter-ego ("chaka" means "woman of fire") by a Yoruba priest while working with the Black Panther movement. Her last name Khan was acquired after a short-lived teen marriage to a musician named Hassan Khan.

Let's Active

This phrase was seen on a t-shirt whose slogan had been incorrectly translated from the original Japanese–it was intended to say "Let's Get Physical".

Lotus Eaters

The Lotus Eaters' name was inspired by a fan who had sardonically signed herself "one of the three million lotus eaters", referring to the number of British unemployed at that time. "Lotus eater" is a term describing someone who is obsessed with sensual enjoyment.

Mamas & Papas

Cass Elliott (b. Ellen Naomi Cohen) was watching an interview with a Hell's Angel who was saying that the tribe call their women "Mamas", so she suggested that, as the group had two girls and two guys, they went with "Papas" too. Elliott changed her name from Ellen Cohen in 1961 to try and break into Broadway as an actress. Michelle Gilliam (b. Holly Michelle Gilliam).

Marilyn Manson

Marilyn Manson are named for vocalist Reverend Marilyn Manson (b. Brian Warner), who named himself after Marilyn Monroe and Charles Manson. The band was originally known as Marilyn Manson & the Spooky Kids, whose lineup all took stage names based on the names of a well-known cultural icon and a serial killer. They included at various times: Olivia Newton-Bundy (from Olivia Newton-John and Ted Bundy; bass–b. Brian Tutunick), Daisy Berkowitz (from Daisy Duke, a character from the TV show *The Dukes of Hazzard* played by Catherine Bach, and David Berkowitz, known as "Son Of Sam"; guitars–b. Scott Putesky), Zsa-Zsa Speck (from Zsa Zsa Gabor and Richard Speck; drums–b. Perry Pandrea), Madonna Wayne Gacy (from Madonna and John Wayne Gacy; keyboards–b. Stephen Bier), Gidget Gein (from *Gidget*, played for TV

by Sandra Dee, and Ed Gein; bass–b. Brad Stewart);
Twiggy Ramirez (from 60s model Twiggy and Richard
Ramirez; bass–b. Jeordie White); Ginger Fish (from Ginger
Rodgers and Albert Fish; drums–b. Kenny Wilson); Sara
Lee Lucas (from Sara Lee, the baked goods brandname,
and Henry Lucas; drums–b. Fred Streithorst).

Milli Vanilli

"Milli" is Turkish for "positive energy", and came about
when the band first started gigging in Munich, which has
a large Turkish population. The band organized "Milli
Night" especially for Turkish customers. Vanilli was added
simply to round off the name.

Osibisa

Osibisa took their name from "osibisaba", the Fanti word
for "highlife". "Highlife" is the name of a form of African
dance music originating in Ghana.

Parliament

Parliament was initially formed in high school as The
Parliaments, which was taken from a brand of cigarettes,
in common with other groups of the time, e.g. The Chester-
fields. Later, the 's' was dropped from the end and the
band became known as Parliament.

Poi Dog Pondering

"Poi dog" is a Hawaiian term for a mongrel dog, or mixed
breed of unknown origin, leader Frank Orrall having come
from Hawaii. The Hawaiian Poi Dog was originally a breed
of hound which lived with Polynesian tribesmen, being fed
on "poi", a paste made from the taro root. Early in the
19th-century they began breeding with other dogs, so that
they were no longer purebred.

Propellerheads

"Propellerheads" is Silicon Valley slang for computer nerds–band members Alex Gifford and Will White had heard the term during a conversation with a Canadian friend.

Queen Latifah

Queen Latifah was born Dana Elaine Owens. She was given the nickname "Latifah" as a child (some references say as a teen) by a cousin who was a Muslim–"latifah" is an Arabic word meaning delicate and sensitive. She added the prefix "Queen" later.

Redbone

Redbone took their name from the Cajun word "rehbon", meaning "half-breed", as all of the original lineup were Native American Indians.

Runrig

Runrig formed as The Run-Rig Dance Band. Run-rig is a type of farming, named from the lines made on the ground by the plough, which was at one time popular on the Scottish island of Skye, where the band was formed. Blair Douglas (accordion) thought of the name when he was a student in Glasgow.

Rush

The name Rush was suggested by a friend of the band, allegedly inspired by a certain recreational product sold around Toronto in the '70s, which, when sniffed, produced a head-rush. Geddy Lee (bass, vocals–b. Gary Lee Weinrib) got his nickname "Geddy" from his Yiddish mother's mispronunciation of his name. Alex Lifeson (b. Alex Zivojinovic), "Lifeson" is taken from the English translation of his Yugoslav surname, literally "son of life".

Scritti Politti

Lead vocalist and guitarist Green was reading an English translation of a book called *Political Writing* by Antonio Gramsci, an Italian Marxist, which had the Italian version of the title, "Scritti Polittici", written on the inside cover. Green decided to drop the "ci" from the end and use Scritti Politti, similar to the famous rock 'n' roll song "Tutti Frutti". Green was born Paul Julian Strohmeyer, but thought his given name Paul was too plain. He thought up his new name while riding a train in summer, when the passing countryside was completely green. He took the surname Gartside after his mother re-married following his father's death.

Shamen

Band member Colin Angus was a keen researcher of Shamanism and the band took their name from this. Shamanism involves the Shaman entering an ecstatic trance in order to achieve some magical speciality, such as healing. Mr C (vocals) was born Richard West, taking the name Chelsea Boy as a CB handle from his love of Chelsea Football Club, later shortening the name to Mr C when he began as an MC.

Sigue Sigue Sputnik

This name was taken from the name of a Moscow street gang, and is Russian for "Burn, burn, Sputnik"–Sputnik was an early Russian satellite. Ex-Boomtown Rats manager Fachtna O'Kelly had seen the name in a *Herald Tribune* article and had shown it to the band.

Sly & The Family Stone

Sly Stone was born Sylvester Stewart, "Sly" being a high-school nickname derived from Sylvester. He formed the band Sly & The Stoners in 1966, which eventually became Sly & The Family Stone. The "Family" part came from the fact that the band included Sly's brother Freddie and his sister Rosemary.

Three Dog Night

This name was taken from an Australian expression for a very cold night, referring to how many dogs it takes to keep warm while sleeping, "three dog nights" being the coldest. The name was suggested by founder member Danny Hutton's girlfriend, June Fairchild, who had seen the term in an article about Australian Aborigines.

Shania Twain

Shania Twain was born Eileen Regina Edwards. Her parents split up and her mother re-married Jerry Twain, an Ojibway Indian. She later adopted the stage-name Shania, an Ojibway word meaning "I'm on my way".

UB40

UB40 were named after the reference number of the old UK Unemployment Benefit form, or "dole card", as it was known, before the benefit was euphemistically relaunched as Jobseeker's Allowance. The name was suggested by a friend of the band, who were all "on the dole" (unem-ployed) at the time.

Wham!

George Michael and Andrew Ridgeley had recorded a demo "Wham Rap", with Wham inspired by the hectic

London night club scene, and the group name came from that. George Michael (vocals) was born Georgios Kyriacos Panayiotou, and took the name Michael from his friend David Austin's dad, who was called Michael Mortimer. Backing singers Pepsi (*b.* Lawrie Damacque and nicknamed "Pepsi" from her bubbly personality) and Shirley (*b.* Shirlie Holliman).

A-List Celebs

Bands and artists whose names were
inspired by famous people

Babe Ruth

Although a British group, they were named after Babe Ruth, the famous American baseball star. The name was changed from the original Shacklock (after guitarist Alan Shacklock), on the release of their first album *First Base* (1973).

Gene Chandler

Gene Chandler was born Eugene Dixon. He took his stage name from his favorite actor, movie star Jeff Chandler, because he thought the combination Gene Chandler had a romantic ring to it.

Dead Kennedys

After rejecting Thalidomide (a drug given to pregnant women in the 1960s which resulted in many deformed children), they settled on a name inspired by the assassinated US politicians, for shock value. Jello Biafra (vocals–b. Eric Boucher)–after first being known as "Occupant", he picked his stage name at random from a note book–"Biafra" was taken from the name of an African country in which thousands of people starved to death following civil war and famine; East Bay Ray Glasser (guitars–b. Ray Pepperell in the East Bay area of the San Francisco Bay); Klaus Flouride (bass–b. Geoffrey Lyall); Ted (drums–b. Bruce Slesinger); D. H. Peligro (drums–b. Darren Henley).

Flesh For Lulu

Flesh For Lulu are an all-vegetarian band, and their name was inspired by seeing pop star **Lulu** buying a burger in a McDonald's fast food restaurant.

Frankie Goes To Hollywood

This name was taken from a magazine headline regarding UK entertainer Frankie Vaughan's future acting plans (not Frank Sinatra as is usually reported). Holly Johnson (vocals–b. William Johnson), took the name "Holly" from a character referenced in Lou Reed's "Walk on the Wild Side"–he was asked for his name on a dance floor and the record happened to be playing at the time.

Gin Blossoms

The Gin Blossoms' name was inspired by a cable TV show about Kenneth Anger's book *Hollywood Babylon II*, which showcased the famous photograph of actor W.C. Fields, highlighting the "gin blossoms" on his face. "Gin blossoms" are caused by ingesting too much sugar, causing the capillaries of the nose to become damaged leading to redness and swelling.

Hues Corporation

Hues Corporation were named after the company owned by eccentric billionaire Howard Hughes. The spelling was changed to avoid legal problems.

Ice-T

Ice-T was born Tracy Morrow, and chose his stage name in honor of pimp-turned-novelist Iceberg Slim, whose poetry Ice-T used to memorize as a youth.

Dean Martin

Dean Martin was born Dino Paul Crocetti. His original stage name was Dino Martini, which he took from a popular Metropolitan Opera star called Nino Martini.

Bandleader Sammy Watkins hired him as a singer and suggested he change his name to Dean Martin.

MC Hammer

MC Hammer was born Stanley Kirk Burrell, and was nicknamed "Little Hammer" while he was a batboy with the Oakland Athletics baseball team, owing to his likeness to baseball legend "Hammerin'" Hank Aaron.

Perpetual Motion

Bands and artists whose names
were inspired by machinery

808 State

808 State were originally called Hit Squad Manchester, but were finally named after their Roland drum machine, model number TR808. The name was chosen to reflect the group's shared interest in dance music, especially Detroit's Techno scene. Band member Gerald Simpson has also made solo recordings as A Guy Called Gerald.

AC/DC

This name was suggested by Margaret, sister of band members Angus and Malcolm Young, after she saw it on her sewing machine. Additionally, Margaret was responsible for suggesting Angus's schoolboy stage outfit. Original vocalist Bon Scott (*b.* Ronald Belford Scott) was born in Scotland but his family moved to Australia when he was young. He was given the nickname "Bonny" (a popular Scottish word) by his Australian schoolmates, which was gradually shortened to Bon.

Acid House

"Acid" refers to the "acidic" popping sounds made by the Roland TR-303 synthesizer, which was used to create the bass lines.

America

Group members Dewey Bunnell and Dan Peek were sons of US servicemen stationed overseas at West Ruislip near London, and the name was inspired by an Americana jukebox which they had seen at the warehouse cafeteria where they both worked.

Buffalo Springfield

This name was seen on a steamroller near early manager Barry Friedman's home–apparently Friedman (later known as Frazier Mohawk) proclaimed the name of the band, stole the sign from the back of the steamroller, took it into his house and nailed it to the wall.

Cars

Cars drummer David Robinson had been saving this name to use for a group. Group members Ric Ocasek (vocals, guitar–b. Richard Otcasek); Benjamin Orr (vocals, bass–b. Benjamin Orzechowski); Elliott Easton (guitar–b. Elliott Shapiro).

Chicago

Chicago were originally named Chicago Transit Authority, a sign seen on the side of a school bus, by their manager James William Guercio. This was later shortened to Chicago after the first album was released, following copyright objections by humorless representatives of the actual Transit Authority.

Echo & The Bunnymen

"Echo" was the name which they had given to the drum machine they used while recording early demos, before they took on a live drummer, while "Bunnymen" was suggested by a friend of the band.

Fuzzbox

Fuzzbox is the shortened version of the full name, which is "We've Got A Fuzzbox And We're Gonna Use It", referring to a statement made by vocalist Maggie Dunne after the band purchased a fuzzbox.

Iron Maiden

Iron Maiden were named after a medieval torture device, which bass player Steve Harris had seen in the movie of *The Man In The Iron Mask* by Alexander Dumas. Bruce Dickinson (vocals–b. Paul Bruce Dickinson); Blaze Bayley (vocals–b. Bayley Cook) adopted the stage name Blaze on joining heavy metal band Wolfsbane, Nicko McBrain (drums–b. Michael McBrain) acquired his nickname as a child, after a teddy bear that he owned called Nicholas.

Kursaal Flyers

The Kursaal Flyers were named after a train which paraded along the seafront advertising Kursaal Amusement Park in the seaside resort town of Southend, UK, where the band was formed.

Lambrettas

Part of the "Mod" revival in Britain in the late 1970s, The Lambrettas took their name from a type of Italian scooter which along with Vespas had been popular with the UK Mods of the '60s.

Mission

The Mission formed out of the remnants of **Sisters of Mercy**, and the name was actually taken from a make of amplifier. Wayne Hussey (guitars, vocals) had wanted to use the name Sisterhood, but ex-colleagues in the Sisters of Mercy prevented this because their fans referred to themselves as "The Sisterhood", and the band sometimes used that name in order to play gigs unannounced. Hussey is quoted by many references as having been born Jerry Lovelock, but his real name is Jerry Wayne Hussey.

Prodigy

Founder member Liam Howlett called himself "The Prodigy" while DJ-ing, taking the name from his synthesizer, a Moog Prodigy. Howlett's alter-ego was subsequently adopted for the band.

Prong

As the band was a three-piece, they decided to take the name "prong" from the three-pronged mains plug used in the United States.

REO Speedwagon

REO stands for Ransom Eli Olds (of Oldsmobile fame), who designed the flat-bed truck known as the Speedwagon. Founder member Neal Doughty was attending a college class on the history of transportation, and one day when he walked into class the words "REO Speedwagon" were written on the blackboard.

Traffic

The name Traffic was thought up by drummer Jim Capaldi, the name coming to him while standing on a street corner watching cars go by.

U2

The U2 is a high-flying US Air Force spy plane. The name was suggested by Steve Rapid, lead singer for another Irish band called The Radiators. Bono was born Paul Hewson–

his stage name, shortened from the original Bono Vox, was inspired by an advert for a hearing aid company in Ireland, actually called Bonavox.

Van Der Graaf Generator

This name was taken from an electrostatic voltage generator developed at Massachussetts Institute of Technology (MIT) and named after its inventor, Robert Jemison Van Der Graaf. The name was suggested by the original drummer, Chris Judge Smith.

Dinner And A Show

Bands and artists whose names were
inspired by food and drink

1910 Fruitgum Co.

Initially known as Jeckell and the Hydes, after group leader Frank Jeckell, the new name came about as Jeckell was searching through a trunk full of old clothes, in the hope of discovering potential stage outfits. The name was seen on a gum wrapper found in the pocket of an old jacket.

Blancmange

Group member Stephen Luscombe (keyboards) was renowned for making rabbit-shaped blancmange, which is a thickened milk pudding (usually molded) popular in Britain.

Blue Oyster Cult

The name Blue Oyster Cult was suggested by the band's manager Sandy Pearlman after opening a can of Blue Point oysters (he had also suggested their previous name, Soft White Underbelly). Pearlman was among the first to use the phrase "Heavy Metal" in reference to music.

Bread

The name Bread was inspired when a Wonder Bread van drove by while the band members were pondering a name.

Bucks Fizz

The band were named by their management team of Andy Hill and Nicola Martin. A "bucks fizz" is a cocktail made from champagne and orange juice. Group members Cheryl Baker (b. Rita Crudgington), Bobby G (b. Robert Gubby).

Cookie Crew

Cookie Crew were originally called Warm Milk and the Cookies Crew, later shortened. MC Remedee (real name Debbie Price); Susie Q (real name Susie Banfield).

Cranberries

This band was originally The Cranberry Saw Us (Cranberry Sauce, geddit?), which was dreamt up by the original vocalist, Niall Quinn (replaced by Dolores O'Riordan), the group name later being shortened to The Cranberries.

Michael Crawford

Michael Crawford was born Michael Patrick Dumble-Smith, but became Michael Ingram when his mother re-married. To avoid confusion with a TV presenter called Michael Ingrams, a member of the actor's union, Equity, which discourages duplication of members' names, he took his stage name at age 15 while touring with an opera company from a Crawford's Biscuits delivery wagon.

Everclear

This name is taken from a brand of 190-proof liquor. Founder member Art Alexakis, a recovered alcoholic, considers it to represent pure, white evil because it looks like water but is almost pure (95%) alcohol.

Green Jelly

Originally formed as Sweet Children, they then changed their name to Green Jello, in reference to the fact that they considered green jello to have the worst flavor. However, they were forced to change to "Green Jelly" after General Foods, the makers of Jell-O, threatened to sue.

Jesus & Mary Chain

Starting life as The Poppy Seeds, they took the name Jesus & Mary Chain from an offer on a breakfast cereal packet, where consumers could send away for a gold Jesus & Mary Chain.

Lemonheads

The Lemonheads' name was suggested by a high school friend of the band after the sour candy of the same name which was introduced in 1962 by the Illinois-based Ferrara Pan Candy Co. Fans would buy them and throw them at the band during live gigs.

Marmalade

Starting out as Dean Ford & The Gaylords, their new name was suggested by their manager, Peter Walsh, who thought of it one day over breakfast. Band members Junior Campbell (b. Willie Campbell), Dean Ford (b. Thomas McAleese).

Ozric Tentacles

The name Ozric Tentacles was originally dreamt up by the band members to be the name of a psychedelic breakfast cereal–they also considered Gilbert Chunks, Desmond Whisps and Malcolm Segments.

Wild Cherry

Wild Cherry were named by original member Bob Parissi, who got the idea while recovering in hospital from an accident, and was inspired by a box of cherry-flavored cough drops.

All Things Bright And Beautiful

Bands and artists whose names were inspired
by things animal, vegetable or mineral

Aqua

Originally called Joyspeed, they changed their name to Aqua, inspired by a poster of an aquarium in their rehearsal room.

Baccara

A Spanish female vocal duo, Baccara was named by RCA record company executive Leon Deane, after the Baccara rose, which is a rare black-colored rose.

Champs

The Champs were named after Champion, the "wonder" horse belonging to Gene Autry, owner of their record label, Challenge Records. Tenor sax player Chuck Rio (*b.* Daniel Flores).

Dinosaur Jr.

Initially formed as Dinosaur and having already released their first album under that name, they added "Jr" to avoid confusion with (and possible legal action from) a band already named The Dinosaurs. The idea for the suffix "Jr" came from the fact that J. Mascis (guitar, vocals–*b.* Joseph Donald Mascis Jr), was himself a "Junior"; Murph (drums–*b.* Emmitt Murphy).

Eek-A-Mouse

Eek-A-Mouse was born Ripton Joseph Hylton. His stage name is taken from the name of a racehorse on which he frequently bet and lost, and which only won when he didn't bet on it.

Faith No More

Faith No More initially formed as Faith No Man, named after a greyhound on which they had bet, but was changed on the departure of the original singer, Mike "The Man" Morris. The new name was suggested by a friend of the band, Will Carpmill, based on the fact that "The Man" was "no more".

Bill Haley & The Comets

The Comets were named after Halley's comet, the celestial body that returns to pass by the Earth every 75 years, itself named for 17th-century English astronomer Edmond Halley. The idea was suggested by radio station program director Bob Johnson at WPWA, where Haley worked as a musical director, because of the similarity of the names.

Hollies

Contrary to popular opinion, The Hollies are not named in tribute to **Buddy Holly**. In fact the group's name was inspired by a Christmas decoration made from holly at Graham Nash's house. Allan Clarke (vocals–b. Harold Allan Clarke).

Housemartins

A housemartin is a type of bird common in the UK–the band has been quoted as saying that they never really thought about a name, just one day they became The Housemartins, which is not very helpful to music chroniclers! Stan Cullimore (guitars–b. Ian Cullimore), Norman Cook (bass–b. Quentin Cook–see separate entry for **Fatboy Slim**).

Iron Butterfly

Iron Butterfly were named during the mid 1960s, when it was popular for new groups to adopt insect names, but as they wanted a heavier image they added "iron" as a prefix to "butterfly".

Lobo

Lobo was born Roland Kent Lavoie. His German Shepherd dog, Boo (featured in his hit song "Me And You And A Dog Named Boo") looked like a wolf, and with "Lobo" being Spanish for "wolf" he decided to adopt it as his stage name.

Los Lobos

"Los Lobos" is Spanish for "the wolves"–the band was originally called "Los Lobos del Este Los Angeles", which translates as "The Wolves Of East Los Angeles", after the city where they were formed.

Procol Harum

Procol Harum were named after the registered pedigree name of a Siamese cat, owned by a friend of the band's manager–the manager had told them the name over the telephone, which was how the name ended up being misspellt (the correct spelling is "procul", the phrase meaning "beyond these things" in Latin).

Skunk Anansie

The name Skunk Anansie is derived from two creatures, the well-known skunk and the not-so-well-known "anansie", a mythical spider-man featured in Jamaican folk-stories (correctly spelled "ananse" but pronounced as the band spell it). The two words together don't have a specific meaning, rather they were chosen simply because they sound good together.

Stray Cats

The band started out as The Bob Cats, then changed to The Tom Cats, before eventually settling on The Stray Cats, after being forced to sleep rough and busk on the streets following a move to England. Band members Lee Rocker (*b.* Leon Drucher), Slim Jim Phantom (*b.* Jim McConnell).

T. Rex

T.Rex was an abbreviation of the original group name, Tyrannosaurus Rex (the name of one of the largest predatory dinosaurs), which was chosen by **Marc Bolan** because he had been impressed as a youngster by a skeleton of the dinosaur at London's Natural History Museum. The long version of the name was perpetually shortened to "T. Rex" by producer Tony Visconti in his work diary entries when recording with Tyrannosaurus Rex. Visconti had also suggested the change of name of one of the group's drummers, Bill Legend (*b.* Bill Fyfield), based on Fyfield's previous band, Legend. Original member Steve Peregrin Took was born Steven Ross Porter, and adopted his stage name from a character in J. R. R. Tolkein's fantasy trilogy *The Lord Of The Rings*, although the character's name in the books is actually spelled Peregrine Took with an "e".

Toto

An early myth about the name Toto was that vocalist Bobby Kimball's real name was Robert Toteaux, however this isn't true. The group name was really inspired by the name of the dog in the 1939 movie *The Wizard of Oz*, directed by Victor Fleming. The band were eating dinner and thinking of names, when the suggestion was made that the name should be two syllables. Later that evening, drummer Jeff Porcaro was watching TV when the movie came on, and he heard the dog's name Toto. Another band member later pointed out that "toto" is Latin for "everything", so the name was chosen.

Take Me Out To The Ball Game

Bands and artists whose names were
inspired by sports and games

Bad English

Initially the band was intended to be called "Full Circle", however the name "Bad English" was suggested as an alternative by keyboard player Jonathan Cain. The term "Bad English" is used in the game of Pool, to describe an unsuccessful attempt to put spin on the cue ball.

Five For Fighting

The name Five For Fighting is inspired by the game of ice hockey, where the penalty for fighting is five minutes in the penalty box. It was also used as the name of a sports column in *Inside Hockey* magazine by band member John Ondrasik.

Foghat

"Foghat" was a word made up by singer/guitarist "Lonesome" Dave Peverett and his brother during a childhood game of Scrabble–he had previously tried to persuade Savoy Brown band mate Chris Youlden to adopt the stagename "Luther Foghat". Peverett adopted his stage name "Lonesome" early in his career (initially as Lonesome Dave Jax) to sound more like a bluesman–he had seen a record by Cornelius "Lonesome Sundown" Green in a catalog.

Human League

Band members and former computer programmers Martin Ware and Ian Craig Marsh formed an electronic dance music band (initially called The Future), and took their name from one of the opposing sides in the third of 14 scenarios of a science-fiction game, Starforce, issued in the mid-1970s.

Hüsker Dü

This name was taken from a children's educational board game popular with Minnesotans (where the band was formed) in the 1950s, and is Danish (not Swedish, as is often reported) for "Do you remember?", as in "Do you remember when the snow wasn't here?". Forming in 1979, the name was chosen so as not to be an obvious punk or new wave name.

Kissing The Pink

"Kissing The Pink" was a term used by a sports commentator that was heard by the band members one night while watching snooker on TV. Some sources also refer to the term being a euphemism for cunnilingus. The band subsequently abbreviated their name to KTP.

Smash Mouth

This band's name was inspired by a term coined by American football coach Mike Ditka, who won the 1985 Super Bowl with the Chicago Bears–"Smash-mouth" football was used to describe a particularly physical approach to the game.

St. Etienne

Founder members Pete Wiggs and Bob Stanley were both football fans, and named their group after the French soccer team that was very successful in the 1970s. The team had played in Britain a number of times and the duo were impressed by their fashionable look and impressive green kit. When they were younger, they imagined themselves being in a band called Saint Etienne and that the town (which is close to Lyons in France, and which they have never visited) would be a very exotic place.

Sugar Ray

Initially called Shrinky Dinx, they were forced to change when the producer of the Shrinky Dinks ornament-making set, K&B Innovations Inc., filed a lawsuit against them. Their new name was inspired by Sugar Ray Leonard, who was the favorite boxer of lead vocalist Mark McGrath.

Artificial Intelligence

Bands and artists whose
names were contrived

98 Degrees

98 degrees is the mean temperature of the human body—the band wanted something that would represent the heat of passion, and had rejected other names, including Just Us, Next Issue and Verse Four.

ABC

Lead vocalist Martin Fry was interviewing the other future members about their group, then called Vice Versa, for his fanzine *Modern Drugs*. After he joined the band, they changed their name to ABC because, by adding new members, they were effectively starting from scratch.

Ace Of Base

This name represents the four members of the band being the aces in the base, "base" coming from the fact that their first studio was built in their basement garage. The band was originally known as "Tech Noir", which was the name of a nightclub in the movie *Terminator* (1984).

Allisons

Brian Henry John Alford and Bernard Colin Day took the stagenames John and Bob Allison respectively, masquerading as brothers in an attempt to be the UK equivalent of the Everly Brothers.

B.E.F

B.E.F. stands for British Electric Foundation, which was a production company formed by Martyn Ware and Ian Craig-Marsh on their departure from the **Human League**, and was used as a production vehicle for side projects such as **Heaven 17**.

Bachelors

Originally known as the Harmonichords, The Bachelors were re-named by Decca A&R man Dick Rowe in order to make them appear more accessible to young girls.

Band Aid

Band Aid was a group (band) of celebrity musicians brought together in 1984 to help (aid) the starving in Africa (hence Band Aid, as in the name of the sticking plaster), at the instigation of Boomtown Rats' leader, Bob Geldof.

Blind Faith

The title "Blind Faith" was given by photographer Bob Seidemann to the image that was used for the as-yet unnamed band's first album cover, depicting a young girl holding a rocket ship. **Eric Clapton** decided to also use the name of the picture as the band name.

Gary "US" Bonds

Gary "US" Bonds was born Gary Anderson. His stage name was suggested by local record producer Frank Guida, and his first single was promoted in sleeves bearing the phrase "Buy US Bonds", which had been inspired by a sign in a local (Norfolk, Virginia) store urging Americans to "Buy US (savings) Bonds".

Buckinghams

An American band who at that time were known as The Pulsations, they had won an audition to star in a show on Chicago, Illinois TV station WGN. The station wanted them to jump on the "British Invasion" bandwagon and adopt a more British-sounding name, and their final name was one of a few alternatives suggested by a security guard at the station, named John Opager.

Buggles

The name Buggles was chosen by group member and producer Trevor Horn, who apparently was tired of producing punk bands with clever names but not-so-clever members, and so he decided to pick the most disgusting name possible.

Jimmy Cliff

Jimmy Cliff was born James Chambers, and he adopted his stage name in 1961 when he started recording for Jamaican record label Beverley's, the name representing the heights he aspired to. He later converted to Islam and became known as Naim Bashir.

Cream

The name Cream came from their opinion of themselves as representing the "cream of the crop" of British musicians, at least at the time they were formed by Eric Clapton, Ginger Baker and Jack Bruce in the mid 1960s.

Crusaders

Originally formed as the Modern Jazz Sextet, they then became the Nite Hawks following a suggestion by drummer Nesbert "Stix" Hooper, based on his own initials. After changing yet again to The Jazz Crusaders, they finally dropped the "Jazz" prefix so as not to limit their appeal.

Taylor Dayne

Taylor Dayne was born Leslie Wunderman, and first recorded under the stage name "Leslee". She created her new stage name in collaboration with her record producer, Ric Wake.

Dazz Band

Initially the band was named The Kinsman Dazz Band and was formed by the members of two existing Cleveland bands, Bell Telefunk and the house band at the Kinsman Grill. "Dazz" is an abbreviated form of the term "danceable jazz", a word that was invented by founder member, Bobby Harris. The word "dazz" was also used by the band Brick in their hit 1976 "Dazz", although the term in this case referred to "Disco Jazz", and the Dazz Band apparently did not take their name from the Brick song.

De La Soul

"De La Soul" represents "from the soul" in French–band member David Jolicoeur has French ancestry. Posdnous (b. Kelvin Mercer, Posdnous is his DJ nickname (almost) spelled backwards–"Soundsop"); Trugoy the Dove (b. David Jude Jolicoeur, Trugoy is "yogurt", his favorite food, spelled backwards); Pasemaster Mase (b. Vincent Mason).

Digable Planets

The Digable Planets are named for the band's notion that each individual is a separate planet. Butterfly (b. Ishmael Butler); Ladybug (b. Katrina Lust, replaced by Mary Ann Vieira); DJ: Squibble the Termite (b. Michael Gabredikan), replaced by Doodlebug (b. Craig Irving)–all the band members took their stage names from insect names because insects are typically communal.

Dogs D'Amour

The name Dogs D'Amour represents "dogs of love", "amour" being the French word for love, and was suggested by band member Ned Christie. Tyla (vocals, guitars–b. Timothy John Taylor), Bam Bam (drums–b. Maurice Phillip Rosenthal III), Sleepy Jo Dog (guitars–b. Jo Almedia), Karl (bass–b. Karl Watson), Ned Christie (b. Robert Stoddard).

EMF

EMF is an abbreviation for Epsom Mad Funkers, as shown on the cover of their recent "*Best Of*" compilation. Early stories intimated that it stood for Ecstasy Mother Fuckers, primarily because the B-side of their debut single "Unbelievable" was called "EMF" and included that phrase in the lyrics.

Wayne Fontana

Born Glyn Geoffrey Ellis, he adopted his stage name in honor of Elvis Presley's drummer, DJ Fontana, and not from his record label Fontana Records, as suggested by some sources.

Four Tops

The Four Tops were originally formed as The Four Aims, but changed their name to avoid confusion with the Ames Brothers. When thinking of an alternative, they were asked why they had originally chosen Four Aims, and responded that they were "aiming" for the "top", so the name Four Tops was proposed instead.

Guess Who

The name Guess Who was used by the unknown band Chad Allen & the Expressions when they recorded a version of **Johnny Kidd & The Pirates** "Shakin' All Over", in order to suggest that they were a major British band recording under a pseudonym (this was at the time of the "British Invasion" of the US in the 1960s). Strangely, both names were used on the album of the same name, although "Guess Who?" was written in larger letters than the band's actual name and became their name shortly after. Chad Allen (*b.* Allen Kobel) took the name Chad in honor of The Chad Mitchell Trio.

Its A Beautiful Day

It's A Beautiful Day was put together by future manager Matthew Katz. Katz had previously decided on the band's name, which was inspired by a phrase uttered by a female acquaintance while they were driving together in California.

Japan

The name Japan was chosen in desperation as the still-unnamed band were about to go on for their first gig, and was suggested by vocalist David Sylvian–it was meant to last only until someone had a better idea. Mick Karn (bass–*b.* Anthony Michaelides) was known to his friends as "Mick" from his given surname–Karn was chosen specifically to start with "K", the last letter of his first name, and started out as "Kar"; David Sylvian (vocals, guitars–*b.* David Alan Batt), Steve Jansen (drums–*b.* Steve Batt)

Kiss

Kiss were named by group member Paul Stanley during a brainstorming session with Gene Simmons while driving around, the idea being to sound dangerous and sexy at the same time. Denouncers claimed it stood for "Kids (or Knights) In Satan's Service". Paul Stanley (guitars, vocals–*b.* Stanley Harvey Eisen); Peter Criss (drums–*b.* George Peter John Crisscoula); Ace Frehley (guitars, vocals–*b.* Paul Daniel Frehley), acquired his nickname at high school because he was an "ace" at fixing up his friends with dates; Gene Simmons (bass–*b*. Chaim Witz), first became known as Gene Klein in order to more easily integrate after moving from Israel to the US, Gene being the anglicized form of his first name, before deciding on the name Simmons during a subway ride.

L.L. Cool J

L.L. Cool J was born James Todd Smith, and his stagename represents Ladies Love Cool James–he has been quoted as saying he chose the name to set a goal for him to aim for. He now uses his real name for movie work.

Loverboy

The name Loverboy was proposed by founder member Paul Dean after browsing a fashion magazine, adapting it from the original suggestion of Cover Boy, itself a twist on Cover Girl. Mike Reno (vocals–*b*. Mike Rynoski) took his stage name from a shortened version of his given name.

Mantronix

Mantronix is a combination of the words "man" and "electronics", with a slight change from "cs" to "x" in the spelling at the end. Kurtis Mantronik (*b*. Kurtis Khaleel) is an ex-aerospace engineer; MC Tee (*b*. Toure Embden).

Massive Attack

Mushroom (keyboards–*b*. Andrew Vowles) has said that the band's name represents a "massive attack" of arts. During the 1991 Gulf War, the band considerately shortened their name to Massive. Mushroom acquired his nickname as a result of his incessant playing of the video game Centipede (Hasbro), where the player guides a centipede through a maze of mushrooms. 3-D (vocals–*b*.

Robert DelNaja) was a noted artist prior to joining the group; Daddy G (keyboards–b. Grant Marshall).

MFSB

MFSB was the studio band employed by TSOP (The Sound Of Philadelphia) producers Kenneth Gamble & Leon Huff–MFSB supposedly stands for Mother, Father, Sister, Brother, chosen because they were tight like a family, although a less socially acceptable alternative (Mother Fucker Son of a Bitch) has also been circulated.

Modern Lovers

The name Modern Lovers was chosen by the group's founder Jonathan Richman to reflect the type of songs he was writing, i.e., songs about modern love.

Presidents Of The United States Of America

The band would think up a different name before each new show when they first started out–Chris Ballew (vocals, bass) came up with this name, which was the longest he could think of, and the name stuck.

Queen

Previously called Smile, the name Queen was chosen by Freddie Mercury (vocals, keyboards–b Faroukh Bulsara) as being very grand sounding–Brian May had suggested Grand Dance, while Roger Taylor had proposed The Rich Kids. Mercury picked up the nickname "Freddie" while at high school in India, and chose the last name "Mercury" because, as a Virgo, that was his ruling planet.

Smiths

"The Smiths" was chosen deliberately to sound indefinite and offset bands who took complex names in order to underline their musical style. Johnny Marr (guitars–*b.* John Maher).

Richard Hell & The Voidoids

The word "voidoid" arose out of a game that Richard Hell (*b.* Richard Meyers) and Tom Verlaine (*b.* Tom Miller) played over burgers in a deli on New York's 2nd Avenue, during which they were attaching "oid" to every word they could think of. Hell later used it as the title of his book, *The Voidoid.* Verlaine took his name from the 19th-century French symbolist poet, Paul Verlaine.

Who

The Who were originally known as The High Numbers, "high number" being a Mod term for "style". The name Who was chosen deliberately to be annoying, such that people would ask, "Who's playing tonight?"–"Yes, that's right"–"But who's playing tonight?"!

Just Because

Bands and artists whose names were chosen
at random or have no special significance

Aerosmith

The name Aerosmith was originally believed to have been inspired by the novel *Arrowsmith*, by Sinclair Lewis, but was later confirmed to have been thought up in high school by drummer Joey Kramer. The band also considered "The Hookers" and "Spike Jones" (after the famous comedy dance band leader) as alternatives. Steven Tyler (vocals–b. Stephen Victor Tallarico) changed his last name to Tyler as that was easier to pronounce than Tallarico–he had also used the name Steve Tally; note that he also changed the spelling of his first name. The band once played an impromptu set as The G-Spots in Cambridge, MA in 1995.

Alice Cooper

Alice Cooper was born Vincent Damon Furnier, although initially the name was applied to the band, only later being adopted by Furnier himself. The name "Alice Cooper" has no special significance, although early stories claimed that "Alice Cooper" was the name of a spirit contacted through a Ouija board at his manager Dick Phillips's house. The band was previously called The Nazz, after The Yardbirds' song "The Nazz Are Blue" from *The Yardbirds* (1966), but decided to change when Todd Rundgren named his band The Nazz.

Bay City Rollers

Previously called The Saxons, The Bay City Rollers were renamed after a city in America (Bay City, Michigan), chosen at random from a map of the US by their manager Tam Paton using a pin with his eyes closed! The first attempt landed in Arkansas but they decided to try again, this time with the pin landing in Bay City. The band were into Motown soul music and wanted a name which sounded more American.

Big Country

Although initially thought to have been named after the movie *The Big Country* (1958) starring Gregory Peck, Stuart Adamson revealed that the name had no specific source, and was chosen because it "implied a sense of vastness, open spaces. A sense of new discovery. A sense of ambition."

Blink 182

Blink 182 originally wanted to use the name Blink, but there was already another band using that name in the UK. The band therefore added the number 182, which most references state is how many times Al Pacino's character says the word "fuck" in the movie *Scarface* (1983, directed by Oliver Stone), but which was actually chosen at random.

Byrds

The Byrds were named during a Thanksgiving dinner at their manager Ed Tickner's house. They were all trying to think of a name, and original member Gene Clark suggested The Birdsies. Tickner modified this to Birds, but it was pointed out that "birds" was slang for girls in the UK, so Roger McGuinn suggested that it should be spelled with a "y". McGuinn (guitars, vocals–*b.* James Joseph McGuinn) changed his name after a guru in Indonesia told him that a new name would give him better vibrations, and suggested the letter "R". McGuinn picked Roger from the radio sign-off term.

Charlatans

Another name chosen at random from the dictionary. This British band were known as Charlatans (U.K.) in the US to differentiate them from a 1960s band of the same name.

Chumbawumba

Early in the band's career it was rumored that the name had been seen in a public toilet during a dream by Danbert Nobacon (b. Nigel Hunter)–"Chumba" was the sign on the gents, and "Wumba" on the ladies. The group denies this however, saying the name means nothing, although Nobacon is normally given credit for coming up with the name. Nobacon did not take his name because he is vegan, as is commonly thought–rather he took his name from the old knock-knock joke ("Knock-knock" "Who's there?" "Egbert" "Egbert who?" "Egbert no bacon!"), using Danbert instead of Egbert because he was called "Dan" by his friends. Alice Nutter (vocals, keyboards) was christened Anne, but changed her name because she didn't like being named after Princess Anne–she was known as Mad Anne when the band first started out; Alice Nutter was the name of a woman falsely accused as a witch in Pendle, Lancashire in 1612 and subsequently executed.

Commodores

Yet another name chosen from a dictionary at random, this one by the band's trumpet player, William King, while blindfolded. The band later pointed out that they came close to being called "The Commodes".

Cowboy Junkies

The band wanted something different and attention-grabbing, and the actual choice of words apparently has no significant meaning. Alan Anton (bass–b. Alan Alizojvodic).

Def FX

The band's manager threw a pile of albums in the air, and both a DefJam compilation and a BBC sound effects record landed on top, the name being a combination of those two albums.

Def Leppard

Their original name of Atomic Mass (a chemical term) was changed to Deaf Leopard, which had been the idea of lead singer Joe Elliott while still at school. The spelling was later changed to Def Leppard at the suggestion of original drummer Tony Kenning, although any connection to **Led Zeppelin** as the inspiration for the spelling change is denied by the band.

Erasure

The name Erasure has been variously reported to have been either inspired by the David Lynch movie *Eraserhead* (1976), starring Jack Nance, or selected from a list that had been circulated to friends. In an interview, Vince Clarke confirmed that the name was in fact picked from a list, and also (rather surprisingly) that he didn't like it.

Fatboy Slim

Fatboy Slim is a pseudonym for leader and ex-**Housemartin** Norman Cook, who was born Quentin

Cook, but changed it legally to Norman, the most normal name he could think of, because of its link to the provocative British gay icon, Quentin Crisp. He has said that the name "Fatboy Slim" just came to him out of thin air around 5a.m. one Sunday, although another story has it as being the name of a 1940s Louisiana blues singer once famous for the song "Baby, I Want A Piece Of Your Pie".

Flying Burrito Brothers

The name Flying Burrito Brothers was initially used by bass player Ian Dunlop and drummer Mickey Gauvin of the International Submarine Band after they split from that band, and was suggested by Dunlop. Dunlop had also suggested the International Submarine Band's name, from the "International Silverstream Submarine Band" featured in the *Our Gang* series of movies in the 1930s. They also went by Burrito Brothers and Flying Brothers at various times.

Go-Betweens

Although many sources claim that their name was taken from the 1970 film *The Go-Between*, directed by Joseph Losey and starring Alan Bates and Julie Christie, the band themselves have stated that they just liked the sound of the name rather than having used the movie title as inspiration.

Grass Roots

Dunhill Records songwriters P.F. Sloan (*b.* Phillip Gary Schlein) and Steve Barri (*b.* Steven Barry Lipkin) were asked to write folk-rock music and release it under a pseudonym, for which they chose the name Grass Roots. Later, a band called The Bedouins was recruited to perform as The Grass Roots then, when all but the singer quit, a band called The 13th Floor replaced them.

Heart

Heart was originally formed as an all-male band in the 1960s and were at that time called The Army. They then changed their name to White Heart, before finally shortening to just Heart, all of which took place before either of the Wilson sisters had joined.

Knack

Most references state that the Knack took their name from a cult '60s British movie *The Knack, And How To Get It* (1965) directed by Dick Lester and starring Ray Brooks, **Michael Crawford** and Rita Tushingham. However, band member Doug Fieger, in the cover notes to the compilation album *Retrospective: The Best of The Knack* (1992), says that the name resulted from a dictionary search after the discovery that a band with their originally planned name already existed.

Billy J. Kramer

Billy J. Kramer was born William Howard Ashton, and chose Kramer at random from the telephone directory. Fellow Liverpool native John Lennon suggested adding the "J" in reference to Lennon's mother Julia and newborn son Julian.

Mitch Ryder & The Detroit Wheels

Mitch Ryder was born William Levise, and his stagename was selected at random from the phone book. The group name "Detroit Wheels" was chosen to sound contemporary.

Nine Inch Nails

Some sources say that this name has a biblical inspiration, i.e. the length of the nails used to crucify Jesus Christ. However, leader Trent Reznor has said that he just wanted a name that sounded tough and the name has no special significance.

Pixies

The Pixies' name was chosen by guitarist Joey Santiago at random from the dictionary. Band member Black Francis was born Charles Michael Kitteridge Thompson IV, Francis being an old family name.

R.E.M.

Although this is the abbreviation for "Rapid Eye Movement", a phenomenon that occurs during dreaming, the use of the term by the band has no hidden meaning, being picked at random from the dictionary.

Replacements

Originally known as The Impediments, the band agreed to step in for another that failed to show at a gig. Leader Paul Westerberg, when asked who they were, said: "We're the replacements". They were known to their fans as The 'Mats, an abbreviated form of the corrupted name "Replacemats".

Runaways

The name Runaways was suggested by the band's producer Kim Fowley, whose original idea it was to form an all-female teen rock band. Jackie Fox (bass–b. Jacqueline Fuchs); Sandy West (drums–b. Sandy Pesavento); Micki Steele (b. Sue Thomas).

Shalamar

The name Shalamar was originally a covername used to issue the single "Uptown Festival" by producers Dick Griffey (also booking agent for the US TV show Soul Train) and Simon Sousson. A real band was later put together following the song's success.

Smashing Pumpkins

Leader Billy Corgan chose this name as something he would like to call a band, even before the band came together. The word "smashing" is used here in the British slang sense of the word, meaning great, good-looking, sexy.

Supergrass

This name was shortened from the original Theodore Supergrass, made up by Danny Goffey (drums). It was initially intended that it would be used as an alter ego so that they wouldn't have to give interviews.

Supremes

The name "Supremes" was chosen by original vocalist Florence Ballard from a list supplied by Motown receptionist and songwriter Janie Bradford.

Television

The name Television was suggested by bandmember **Richard Hell** (b. Richard Meyers), and coincided with the initials of **Tom Verlaine**'s adopted name.

Wishbone Ash

The group's manager, Miles Copeland, (brother of **Police** drummer Stewart Copeland) came up with two lists of potential names, from one the band chose "wishbone", and from the other they chose "ash".

And Finally...

Artists who have changed
their names for the stage

JOHNNY ACE was born John Marshall Alexander Jr.

BALTIMORA was born Jimmy McShane.

BASEHEAD was born Michael Ivey. He also recorded as B.Y.O.B. (Bastard Youth Of Basehead).

WILLIAM BELL was born William Yarborough.

BELOUIS SOME was born Neville Keighley.

BOMB THE BASS was born Tim Simenon.

LOU BUSCH was born Joe Carr (*AKA* Joe "Fingers" Carr).

FREDDY CANNON was born Frederick Anthony Picariello. Early demos were recorded as Freddy Karmon.

VIKKI CARR was born Florencia Bisenta de Casillas Martinez Cardona.

TONY CHRISTIE was born Anthony Fitzgerald.

RANDY CRAWFORD was born Veronica Crawford.

DAVID & JONATHAN was a recording alias for songwriting duo Roger Greenaway and Roger Cook.

KIKI DEE was born Pauline Matthews.

DISCO TEX was born Joseph Montanez Jr, *AKA* Sir Monti Rock III.

DJ SHADOW was born Josh Davis.

DMX (Dark Man X) was born Earl Simmons

SHEENA EASTON was born Sheena Shirley Orr.

EMINEM was born Marshall Mathers.

DAVID ESSEX was born David Cook.

FALCO was born Johann Hoelzel, later taking the stage name John Di Falco.

FREDDY FENDER was born Baldomar G. Huerta.

FLAVOR FLAV was born William Drayton.

FLO & EDDIE is short for The Phlorescent Leech & Eddie, alias ex-Turtles Marc Volman and Howard Kaylan.

EMILE FORD was born Emile Sweetman.

LITA FORD was born Rosanna Ford.

KINKY FRIEDMANN was born Richard Freidmann.

BLIND BOY FULLER was born Fulton Allen.

CRYSTAL GAYLE was born Brenda Webb (she is the sister of Loretta Lynn).

GINUWINE was born Elgin Lumpkin.

GARY GLITTER was born Paul Gadd. He also considered other stage names including Terry Tinsel, Stanley Sparkle and Vicky Vomit! He recorded briefly under the pseudonym Rubber Bucket.

DOBIE GRAY was born Leonard Victor Ainsworth III.

GUITAR SHORTY was born David William Kearney.

GUITAR SLIM was born Eddie Jones.

ICE CUBE was born O'Shea Jackson.

JAM MASTER JAY was born Jason Mizell.

JIMMY JAM (producer) was born James Harris III.

RICK JAMES was born James Johnson.

JAY Z was born Shawn Carter.

JELLYBEAN was born John Benitez.

EDEN KANE was born Richard Sarstedt (brother of Peter and Robin Sarstedt).

KEITH was born James Keefer.

BEN E KING was born Benjamin Earl Nelson.

CAROLE KING was born Carole Klein.

KRS-ONE was born Lawrence Krisna "Kris" Parker.

DENNY LAINE (Moody Blues and Wings) was born Brian Hines.

FRANKIE LAINE was born Frank LoVecchio.

KETTY LESTER was born Revoyda Frierson.

HUEY LEWIS was born Hugh Cregg III.

LIGHTNIN' SLIM was born Otis Hicks

LORETTA LYNN was born Loretta Webb, and is the sister of Crystal Gayle.

BARRY MANILOW was born Barry Alan Pinkus.

MARTIKA was born Martha Marrero.

JOHN MARTYN was born Iain McGeachy.

C.W. MCCALL was born William Fries; he created the character of C.W. McCall while working in advertising.

SCOTT McKENZIE was born Philip Blondheim.

GEORGE MICHAEL was born Georgios Kyriacos Panayiotou.

ROBERT MILES ws born Robert Concina.

MICKIE MOST (producer) was born Michael Peter Hayes.

NOTORIOUS B.I.G. was born Christopher Wallace, *AKA* Biggie Smalls, 6' 3" and 280lbs (20 stones).

BILLY OCEAN was born Leslie Sebastian Charles.

MICA PARIS was born Michelle Walden.

PEBBLES was born Perri McKissack.

PROFESSOR LONGHAIR was born Roy Byrd.

MA RAINEY was born Gerturde Pridgett.

SHABBA RANKS was born Rexton Fernando Gordon.

REBEL MC was born Michael Alec Anthony West.

SMOKEY ROBINSON was born William Robinson.

HENRY ROLLINS was born Henry Garfield.

LEON RUSSELL was born Hank Wilson.

SAM THE SHAM was born Domingo Samudio.

DAVID SEVILLE was born Ross Bagdasarian, and because he was already an established composer, he changed his name (selecting from several supplied by his record company) for recording as The Chipmunks.

DEE DEE SHARP was born Dione La Rue.

NINA SIMONE was born Eunice Wayman.

SLIM HARPO was born James Moore. He was originally known as Harmonica Slim and is the brother-in-law of Lightnin' Slim.

EDWIN STARR was born Charles Hatcher.

CAT STEVENS was born Steven Demetri Giorgious, although since converting to Islam he is now known as Yusef Islam.

SYREETA was born Rita Wright.

TAJ MAHAL was born Henry St. Claire Fredericks Williams.

JOE TEX was born Joseph Arrington Jr. in Rogers, TX.

JOHNNY THUNDER was born Gil Hamilton.

TINY TIM was born Herbert Khaury.

TWINKLE was born Lynn Ripley.

DICKIE VALENTINE was born Richard Brice.

VANILLA ICE was born Robert van Winkle.

FRANKIE VAUGHAN was born Frank Abelson.

SCOTT WALKER was born Noel Scott Engel.

DINAH WASHINGTON was born Ruth Lee Jones.

SONNY BOY WILLIAMSON: there were two Sonny Boy Williamsons, the first was born John Lee Williamson, and the second Rice Miller.

STEVIE WONDER was born Steveland Judkins Morris, and started out age 12 billed as Little Stevie Wonder.

YA KID K was born Barbara Kamosi Maoso Duogi.

ZODIAC MINDWARP was born Mark Manning.

Index

Entries are shown in upper case and bold typeface (page numbers)

Links

I have not attempted to cite in the text all of the sources which I researched in the preparation of this book, owing to the fact that the entries are drawn from multiple sources as I attempted to perfect each one. However, the following reference books were helpful when I first started this project:

Illustrated New Musical Express Encyclopedia of Rock, Compiled by Nick Logan & Bob Woffinden (Salamander Books)

Guinness Book of Rock Stars, edited by Daffyd Rees and Luke Crampton with Barry Lazell (Guinness Publishing)

Guinness Rockopedia, David Roberts (Guinness Publishing)

Penguin Encyclopedia of Popular Music, edited by Donald Clarke (Penguin Books)

Billboard Book of Top 40 Hits, Joel Whitburn (Billboard Books)

Additionally, with the increasing popularity of the World Wide Web the following music reference sites appeared time and again during my various researches:

45-rpm.org.uk

artistdirect.com

bbc.co.uk/entertainment/popmusic

borderlinebooks.com/uk6070s/tapestry.html–"The Tapestry of Delights", by Vernon Joynson

centrohd.com/bio/artists

classicbands.com

en.wikipedia.org/–"Wikipedia"

hiponline.com

history-of-rock.com

launch.yahoo.com/

livedaily.com

mtv.com

musicweb.uk.net–"MusicWeb Encyclopedia of Popular Music", edited by Donald Clarke

rockintown.com

roughguides.com/music/rock.html–"The Rough Guide to Rock", edited by Peter Buckley

scaruffi.com/music.html–"The History of Rock Music"

theiceberg.com

vh1.com

Cidermill Books

Visit us on the web at
www.cidermillbooks.com